TEACHER'S PET PUBLICATIONS

LITPLAN TEACHER PACK
for
Izzy, Willy-Nilly
based on the book by
Cynthia Voigt

Written by
Debra Lemieux

© 2006 Teacher's Pet Publications
All Rights Reserved

This LitPlan for
Izzy, Willy-Nilly
has been brought to you by Teacher's Pet Publications, Inc.

Copyright Teacher's Pet Publications 2006

Only the student materials in this unit plan (such as worksheets, study questions, and tests) may be reproduced multiple times for use in the purchaser's classroom.

For any additional copyright questions,
contact Teacher's Pet Publications.

www.tpet.com

TABLE OF CONTENTS – *Izzy, Willy-Nilly*

Introduction	5
Unit Objectives	7
Reading Assignment Sheet	8
Unit Outline	9
Study Questions (Short Answer)	13
Quiz/Study Questions (Multiple Choice)	22
Pre-reading Vocabulary Worksheets	39
Lesson One (Introductory Lesson)	63
Nonfiction Assignment Sheet	83
Oral Reading Evaluation Form	67
Writing Assignment 1	70
Writing Assignment 2	87
Writing Assignment 3	92
Writing Evaluation Form	71
Vocabulary Review Activities	90
Extra Writing Assignments/Discussion ?s	88
Unit Review Activities	93
Unit Tests	97
Unit Resource Materials	131
Vocabulary Resource Materials	165

A FEW NOTES ABOUT THE AUTHOR
Cynthia Voigt

VOIGT, CYNTHIA (born 1942), U.S. author, born on February 25, 1942, in Boston, Mass. Voigt writes fiction for children and young adults. She has been praised for her strong characterizations and for her careful style of writing.

Voigt studied at Smith College, receiving a B. A. in 1963, and taught high school English in Maryland from 1965 to 1967. She taught at The Key School in Annapolis beginning in 1968 and was chairman of the English department from 1971 to 1979. From 1981 she taught part time and continued as department chairman. Her first novel, *Homecoming* (1981), was nominated for an American Book Award. Other novels included *Tell Me If The Lovers Are Losers* (1982), which told the story of several girls of widely different backgrounds who learn from one another as they form a volleyball team in college; *Dicey's Song* (1982), which won a Newbery Medal; and *The Calendar Papers* (1983). *Homecoming* and *Dicey's Song* tell of a young girl named Dicey and her siblings.

--Courtesy of Compton's Learning Company

INTRODUCTION

This LitPlan has been designed to develop students' reading, writing, thinking, and language skills through exercises and activities related to *Izzy, Willy-Nilly*. It includes 22 lessons, supported by extra resource materials.

The introductory lesson offers students an opportunity to reflect upon the causes and effects of peer pressure, an important issue addressed in the book. Following the introductory activity, students are given a transition to explain how the activity relates to the book they are about to read. Following the transition, students are given the materials they will be using during the unit. At the end of the lesson, students begin the pre-reading work for the first reading assignment.

The reading assignments are approximately 30 pages each; some are a little shorter while others are a little longer. Students have approximately 15 minutes of pre-reading work to do prior to each reading assignment. This pre-reading work involves reviewing the study questions for the assignment and doing some vocabulary work for 8 to 10 vocabulary words they will encounter in their reading.

The study guide questions are fact-based questions; students can find the answers to these questions right in the text. These questions come in two formats: short answer or multiple choice. The best use of these materials is probably to use the short answer version of the questions as study guides for students (since answers will be more complete), and to use the multiple choice version for occasional quizzes.

The vocabulary work is intended to enrich students' vocabularies as well as to aid in the students' understanding of the book. Prior to each reading assignment, students will complete a two-part worksheet for approximately 8 to 10 vocabulary words in the upcoming reading assignment. Part I focuses on students' use of general knowledge and contextual clues by giving the sentence in which the word appears in the text. Students are then to write down what they think the words mean based on the words' usage. Part II nails down the definitions of the words by giving students dictionary definitions of the words and having students match the words to the correct definitions based on the words' contextual usage. Students should then have an understanding of the words when they meet them in the text.

After each reading assignment, students will go back and formulate answers for the study guide questions. Discussion of these questions serves as a review of the most important events and ideas presented in the reading assignments.

After students complete reading the work, there is a vocabulary review lesson which pulls together all of the fragmented vocabulary lists for the reading assignments and gives students a review of all of the words they have studied.

Following the vocabulary review, a lesson is devoted to the extra discussion questions/writing assignments. These questions focus on interpretation, critical analysis and personal response, employing a variety of thinking skills and adding to the students' understanding of the novel.

There is a group theme project in this unit. Student groups research a selected disability and apply what they learned toward the creation of a school-based accessibility checklist. The checklist raises awareness of the challenges people with disabilities face.

There are three writing assignments in this unit, each with the purpose of informing, persuading, or having students express personal opinions. In the first assignment, students must evaluate the pros and cons of a decision the main character must address. Students write persuasive letters to encourage the character to select their stated positions. The second writing assignment asks students to consider the future of selected characters by writing an epilogue for the book. In the third assignment, students write to inform others of ways to help the main character assimilate and succeed.

There is a nonfiction reading assignment that also ties in with the group assignment. Students must read nonfiction articles, books, etc. to gather information about living with disabilities.

The review lesson pulls together all of the aspects of the unit. The teacher is given four or five choices of activities or games to use which all serve the same basic function of reviewing all of the information presented in the unit.

The unit test comes in two formats: multiple choice or short answer. As a convenience, two different tests for each format have been included. There is also an advanced short answer unit test for advanced students.

There are additional support materials included with this unit. The Unit Resource Materials section includes suggestions for an in-class library, crossword and word search puzzles related to the novel, and extra worksheets. There is a list of bulletin board ideas which gives the teacher suggestions for bulletin boards to go along with this unit. In addition, there is a list of extra class activities the teacher could choose from to enhance the unit or as a substitution for an exercise the teacher might feel is inappropriate for his/her class. Answer keys are located directly after the reproducible student materials throughout the unit. The Vocabulary Resource Materials section includes similar worksheets and games to reinforce the vocabulary words.

The level of this unit can be varied depending upon the criteria on which the individual assignments are graded, the teacher's expectations of his/her students in class discussions, and the formats chosen for the study guides, quizzes and test. If teachers have other ideas/activities they wish to use, they can usually easily be inserted prior to the review lesson.

The student materials may be reproduced for use in the teacher's classroom without infringement of copyrights. No other portion of this unit may be reproduced without the written consent of Teacher's Pet Publications, Inc.

UNIT OBJECTIVES – *Izzy, Willy-Nilly*

1. Through reading Voigt's *Izzy, Willy-Nilly*, students will consider the consequences of peer pressure.

2. Students will demonstrate their understanding of the text on four levels: factual, interpretive, critical and personal.

3. Students will become aware of the challenges people with disabilities face.

4. Students will be given the opportunity to practice reading aloud and silently to improve their skills in each area.

5. Students will answer questions to demonstrate their knowledge and understanding of the main events and characters in *Izzy, Willy-Nilly* as they relate to the author's theme development.

6. Students will enrich their vocabularies and improve their understanding of the novel through the vocabulary lessons prepared for use in conjunction with the novel.

7. The writing assignments in this unit are geared to several purposes:
    a. To have students demonstrate their abilities to inform, to persuade, or to express their own personal ideas
        Note: Students will demonstrate the ability to write effectively to inform by developing and organizing facts to convey information. Students will demonstrate the ability to write effectively to persuade by selecting and organizing relevant information, establishing an argumentative purpose, and by designing an appropriate strategy for an identified audience. Students will demonstrate the ability to write effectively to express personal ideas by selecting a form and its appropriate elements.
    b. To check the students' reading comprehension
    c. To make students think about the ideas presented by the novel
    d. To encourage logical thinking
    e. To provide an opportunity to practice good grammar and improve students' use of the English language.

8. Students will read aloud, report, and participate in large and small group discussions to improve their public speaking and personal interaction skills.

READING ASSIGNMENT SHEET – *Izzy, Willy-Nilly*

Date Assigned	Chapters Assigned	Completion Date
	1-2	
	3-4	
	5-6	
	7-8	
	9-10	
	11-12	
	13-14	
	15-17	
	18-19	
	20-22	

UNIT OUTLINE – *Izzy, Willy-Nilly*

1 Introduction	2 Thank Yous Unit Materials	3 PVR Ch 1-2	4 ?s 1-2 PVR Ch 3-4	5 ?s 3-4 Writing #1 PV 5-6
6 Vocab 5-6 Read 5-6	7 ?s 5-6 PVR Ch 7-8 Project Intro	8 ?s 7-8 Living With Disabilities PVR 9-10	9 Quiz 1-10 ?s 9-10 PVR Ch 11-12	10 ?s 11-12 Disabilities Act PVR Ch 13-14
11 ?s 13-14 Disabling Diseases PVR Ch 15-17	12 ?s 15-17 Research Reports PVR 18-19	13 ?s 18-19 School Evaluation PVR 20-22	14 ?s 20-22 Writing #2	15 Extra Discussion ?s
16 Extra Discussion ?z	17 Vocabulary Review	18 Writing #3	19 Unit Review	20 Unit Test

Key: P = Preview Study Questions V = Vocabulary Work R = Read

STUDY GUIDE QUESTIONS

SHORT ANSWER STUDY GUIDE QUESTIONS - Izzy, Willy-Nilly

Chapters 1 and 2
1. In what ways is Izzy considered nice?
2. Who is Marco Griggers?
3. What does the policeman ask Izzy?
4. What does Izzy's mother say that makes Izzy want to laugh?
5. Once Izzy falls asleep, what does she dream about?
6. Why did Izzy's parents not want her to go out with Marco?
7. In what state of mind is Marco right before he drives Izzy home?
8. What two tragic events occur at the end of chapter two?

Chapters 3 and 4
1. Who is little Izzy?
2. What school activity does Izzy miss?
3. Who is Rosamunde Webber?
4. Why does Izzy's best friend, Suzy, call Izzy from the pay phone at school?
5. What is odd about the visit from Izzy's friends, Suzy, Lisa, and Lauren?
6. At the end of chapter four, what does Izzy look at?

Chapters 5 and 6
1. Right after Izzy realizes her leg has been amputated, who shows up and why?
2. Who has not sent Izzy a get-well card, or anything?
3. When Izzy wakes up in the darkness of the night, what does she do?
4. Why does Izzy's brother, Jack, not visit her in the hospital?
5. According to Dr. Epstein, how long will it be before Izzy can return home?
6. Instead of telling her parents she is feeling depressed, what does Izzy tell her parents?
7. What was Izzy's guess about why Suzy and Lisa had visited?

Chapters 7 and 8
1. What question does everyone ask Izzy?
2. What does Rosamunde Webber say when she first sees Izzy?
3. Who does Izzy's mother see crying at the hospital?
4. What does Izzy ask Dr. Epstein?
5. Who does Dr. Epstein compare Izzy to and why?
6. How does Rosamunde respond to Izzy's telephone call from her brother Jack?

Izzy Short Answer Study Questions page 2

Chapters 9 and 10
1. What did Rosamunde hang on the hospital room wall?
2. Where are Izzy's parents going dressed in their formal wear?
3. According to Rosamunde, what other meanings for "nice" are there?
4. When Joel visited Izzy, why did he not allow Jack to come with him?
5. What is the first thing Izzy wants to do when she gets home?
6. Mrs. Lingard thinks Rosamunde must feel uncomfortable. Why?
7. Rosamunde knows Izzy is lying about the details of the accident. Instead of lying about the accident, what does Rosamunde offer to tell her father, the policeman?
8. When Izzy returns home, what has changed?

Chapter 11 and 12
1. Prior to Izzy's return home, how had Francie often felt toward Izzy?
2. What did Mrs. Lingard remove from Izzy's closet?
3. Izzy figures out that Suzy is wearing whose letter sweater?
4. Among Izzy's friends, who possesses "the strong personality?"
5. When Rosamunde stops by Izzy's house to pick up the things she'd loaned, what makes her laugh?
6. According to Rosamunde, has Marco learned his lesson?
7. Who annoys Mrs. Lingard by honking the car horn?

Chapters 13 and 14
1. What homework assignment does Izzy have trouble understanding?
2. Who does not return Izzy's telephone calls?
3. Who are fighting in the first scene of Romeo and Juliet?
4. What makes Mrs. Jones, Izzy's physical therapy nurse, smile?
5. Izzy does not want to get a hair cut. Why?
6. How does Suzy describe Rosamunde?
7. What game is the center of a boys versus girls competition?
8. According to Joel, what does Jack underestimate in Izzy?

Chapters 15 - 17
1. Who pays Izzy an unexpected visit?
2. Izzy has been asked to join what selective school activity?
3. What does Adelia suggest Izzy wear?
4. What does Izzy want to borrow from Francie?
5. How does Izzy respond when Rosamunde asks, "What do you think of me?"
6. Why is Mrs. Lingard a little concerned about Rosamunde?

Izzy Short Answer Study Questions page 3

Chapters 18 and 19
1. What is Mr. Lingard thinking of putting in the backyard?
2. How does Izzy respond to Francie's complaint that Izzy gets everything just because she's crippled?
3. What scares Izzy about her return to school?
4. According to Rosamunde, why has Suzy "dropped" Marco Griggers?
5. What does Izzy tell Rosamunde and make her promise not to tell anyone?
6. How does Rosamunde get Izzy to go to school?

Chapters 20-22
1. Excluding Izzy, how many people are on the school newspaper staff?
2. While at school, what makes Izzy cry?
3. What does Izzy want to give Rosamunde for Christmas?
4. How does Izzy spend New Year's Eve?
5. At Lisa's party, how does Lauren act toward Izzy?
6. What does Tony Marcel forget that causes "little Izzy" to do an impossible back flip?
7. When Izzy sees Marco and Georgie Lowe together, what question does she ask Georgie?

ANSWER KEY SHORT ANSWER STUDY GUIDE QUESTIONS – *Izzy, Willy-Nilly*

Chapters 1 and 2

1. In what ways is Izzy considered nice?
    Examples include: easy to get along with, fun to have around, did the work she was told to do, tried to make peace in quarrels, liked people etc.

2. Who is Marco Griggers?
    He is a boy Izzy had been out with the night of the accident.

3. What does the policeman ask Izzy?
    "Would you have been driving? Or messing around with the steering wheel? I mean, if you were steering and he was working the accelerator?"

4. What does Izzy's mother say that makes Izzy want to laugh?
    "I'd rather stay, but–I'll be no use to anyone if I don't get some sleep. A good mother would stay."

5. Once Izzy falls asleep, what does she dream about?
    In her dream, she sits in the front seat of a car that seems to be going slowly, but actually is going too fast. She screams and tries to push herself away from an approaching big tree while the back of the seat traps her.

6. Why did Izzy's parents not want her to go out with Marco?
    They did not know him. He hadn't been a friend of the twins'. Most of the other kids at the party would be older.

7. In what state of mind is Marco right before he drives Izzy home?
    He is drunk and angry.

8. What two tragic events occur at the end of chapter two?
    Marco swerves off the road and into a tree. Dr. Carstair's amputates half of Izzy's right leg.

Chapters 3 and 4

1. Who is little Izzy?
    She is a miniaturized version of Izzy that Izzy envisions in her mind.

2. What school activity does Izzy miss?
    She misses Latin Club.

3. Who is Rosamunde Webber?
    Rosamunde is a smart girl at school who shares a lot of the same classes as Izzy but does not "fit in."

4. Why does Izzy's best friend, Suzy, call Izzy from the pay phone at school?
   Suzy wants to tell Izzy that Marco is sorry and worried. He hopes that Izzy won't try to get even with him because everyone at the party could get in trouble too.

5. What is odd about the visit from Izzy's friends, Suzy, Lisa, and Lauren?
   They do not have anything to talk about.

6. At the end of chapter four, what does Izzy look at?
   Izzy looks at what Suzy, Lisa, and Lauren had been staring at, her legs.

Chapters 5 and 6
1. Right after Izzy realizes her leg has been amputated, who shows up and why?
   A nurse arrives to massage her legs.

2. Who has not sent Izzy a get-well card, or anything?
   Marco has not sent anything.

3. When Izzy wakes up in the darkness of the night, what does she do?
   She cries.

4. Why does Izzy's brother, Jack, not visit her in the hospital?
   Her brother Joel implies Jack has not visited because of a girl, but Izzy believes Jack is lying to her. She wonders if something terrible happened to Jack. Later, she wonders if he didn't want to look at her.

5. According to Dr. Epstein, how long will it be before Izzy can return home?
   Dr. Epstein said it would not be for at least a week more, and probably closer to two weeks.

6. Instead of telling her parents she is feeling depressed, what does Izzy tell her parents?
   She tells them she is tired.

7. What was Izzy's guess about why Suzy and Lisa visited?
   "Somebody had given them an earful," and "they'd been forced to come."

Chapters 7 and 8
1. What question does everyone ask Izzy?
   How are you?

2. What does Rosamunde Webber say when she first sees Izzy?
   "You look terrible."

3. Who does Izzy's mother see crying at the hospital?
   Rosamunde was crying.

4. What does Izzy ask Dr. Epstein?
    She asks if she can watch when he changes the bandages on her leg.

5. Who does Dr. Epstein compare Izzy to and why?
    He compares Izzy to the character Dora in Dickens' *David Copperfield* because Izzy's eyes are so big.

6. How does Rosamunde respond to Izzy's telephone call from her brother Jack?
    Rosamunde grabs the phone from Izzy, confronts Jack, and makes him hang up.

Chapters 9 and 10
1. What did Rosamunde hang on the hospital room wall?
    She hangs a batik cloth covered with animals that her mother had made.

2. Where are Izzy's parents going dressed in their formal wear?
    They are attending a formal dinner dance.

3. According to Rosamunde, what other meanings for "nice" are there?
    She says other meanings would be, "fine, delicate, precise, like a nice distinction, or a nice point."

4. When Joel visited Izzy, why did he not allow Jack to come with him?
    Jack was too angry.

5. What is the first thing Izzy wants to do when she gets home?
    She wants to order a pizza with double cheese, sausage, green peppers and mushrooms.

6. Mrs. Lingard thinks Rosamunde must feel uncomfortable. Why?
    She thinks Rosamunde must feel uncomfortable because of the way Rosamunde looks. "With that nose, and hair? And her figure?"

7. Rosamunde knows Izzy is lying about the details of the accident. Instead of lying about the accident, what does Rosamunde offer to tell her father, the policeman?
    "I can say you said you couldn't tell them anything more than you already have."

8. When Izzy returns home, what has changed?
    Her parents' bedroom, located on the first floor, is now her bedroom.

Chapters 11 and 12
1. Prior to Izzy's return home, how had Francie often felt toward Izzy?
    She had been jealous of Izzy because Izzy was prettier and easy to get along with.

2. What did Mrs. Lingard remove from Izzy's closet?
    She removed all of Izzy's right shoes.

3. Izzy figures out that Suzy is wearing whose letter sweater?
    Suzy is wearing Marco's letter sweater.

4. Among Izzy's friends, who possesses "the strong personality?"
    Suzy has the strong personality.

5. When Rosamunde stops by Izzy's house to pick up the things she'd loaned, what makes her laugh?
    The line of left foot shoes in Izzy's closet makes Rosamunde laugh.

6. According to Rosamunde, has Marco learned his lesson?
    No, Rosamunde thinks he can't even learn from experience. "Unless he's lying, he's still driving around more drunk than he should be."

7. Who annoys Mrs. Lingard by honking the car horn?
    Mr. Webber honks the horn.

Chapters 13 and 14
1. What homework assignment does Izzy have trouble understanding?
    She has trouble understanding English, specifically Shakespeare's words and the *Romeo and Juliet* paraphrasing assignments.

2. Who does not return Izzy's telephone calls?
    Suzy doesn't return Izzy's calls.

3. Who are fighting in the first scene of Romeo and Juliet?
    The servants are fighting.

4. What makes Mrs. Jones, Izzy's physical therapy nurse, smile?
    Izzy tells her that she was thinking about *Romeo and Juliet*.

5. Izzy does not want to get a hair cut. Why?
    Izzy is not ready to face the public because people will stare at her.

6. How does Suzy describe Rosamunde?
    Examples include: like a leech and not cool at all, desperate to have friends, and acting big because she had helped Izzy.

7. What game is the center of a boys versus girls competition?
    Izzy, her siblings, and Rosamunde play a game of Trivial Pursuit.

8. According to Joel, what does Jack underestimate in Izzy?
    He underestimates her brains.

Chapters 15 - 17

1. Who pays Izzy an unexpected visit?
   Tony Marcel and Deborah visit Izzy.

2. Izzy has been asked to join what selective school activity?
   Tony invited her to join the school newspaper staff.

3. What does Adelia suggest Izzy wear?
   Adelia suggests that Izzy could wear trousers, pinned up in the back.

4. What does Izzy want to borrow from Francie?
   Izzy wants to borrow Francie's colored pens.

5. How does Izzy respond when Rosamunde asks, "What do you think of me?"
   Izzy responds, "You are definitely weird, but good weird."

6. Why is Mrs. Lingard a little concerned about Rosamunde?
   Mrs. Lingard thinks Rosamunde is not Izzy's kind of friend because Rosamunde is "so different, in everything, her attitudes, her background, her values." She also thinks Rosamunde is a "clinger."

Chapters 18 and 19

1. What is Mr. Lingard thinking of putting in the backyard?
   Mr. Lingard is thinking about putting in a swimming pool.

2. How does Izzy respond to Francie's complaint that Izzy gets everything just because she's crippled?
   She responds by saying, "Every cloud has a silver lining."

3. What scares Izzy about her return to school?
   She is scared of facing all the people, especially Marco Griggers.

4. According to Rosamunde, why has Suzy "dropped" Marco Griggers?
   Suzy has found someone better, a college boy.

5. What does Izzy tell Rosamunde and make her promise not to tell anyone?
   Izzy tells Rosamunde the truth about what happened the night of the accident.

6. How does Rosamunde get Izzy to go to school?
   She shows up at Izzy's house on Thursday morning and says that Izzy needs someone to carry her books.

Chapters 20-22

1. Excluding Izzy, how many people are on the school newspaper staff?
    There are fifteen other staff members.

2. While at school, what makes Izzy cry?
    Someone quickly cuts past her, and she falls on her face. Feeling humiliated, she waits until everyone is gone, except Rosamunde, and wails.

3. What does Izzy want to give Rosamunde for Christmas?
    Izzy wants to give Rosamunde a haircut for Christmas.

4. How does Izzy spend New Year's Eve?
    She spends New Year's Eve babysitting Francie.

5. At Lisa's party, how does Lauren act toward Izzy?
    If Izzy moved into a room where Lauren was, Lauren left the room.

6. What does Tony Marcel forget that causes "little Izzy" to do an impossible back flip?
    Tony forgets to bring Izzy her crutches.

7. When Izzy sees Marco and Georgie Lowe together, what question does she ask Georgie?
    "Are you going to go out with him?"

STUDY GUIDE/QUIZ QUESTIONS – *Izzy, Willy-Nilly*
Multiple Choice Format

<u>Chapters 1 and 2</u>

1. In what ways is Izzy considered nice?
   a. She is easy to get along with, fun to have around, and likes people.
   b. She is a peer counselor and math tutor at her school.
   c. She often baby sits for her parents and neighbors.
   d. She listens well to others and helps them with their problems.

2. Who is Marco Griggers?
   a. A comical television character
   b. A police officer
   c. A person Izzy had been out with the night of the accident
   d. A therapist

3. What does the policeman ask Izzy?
   a. "Who else was in the car?"
   b. "How old are you?"
   c. "Would you have been driving?"
   d. "Where were you before the accident?"

4. What does Izzy's mother say that makes Izzy want to laugh?
   a. "The phone's been ringing off the hook. You must know everyone at school!"
   b. "I'd rather stay, but–I'll be no use to anyone if I don't get some sleep. A good mother would stay."
   c. "The cheerleading squad made up a feel better-get well soon-we miss you cheer. Do you want me to perform it?"
   d. "Do you want me to ask the doctor to bake your favorite dessert?"

5. Once Izzy falls asleep, what does she dream about?
   a. She dreams of never making it to her own surprise party.
   b. She dreams she's unable to walk down a long hallway.
   c. She dreams she is clinging to the side of a cliff.
   d. She dreams she is sitting in the front seat of a car.

6. Why did Izzy's parents not want her to go out with Marco?
   a. The twins did not like him.
   b. He was trouble.
   c. They did not know him.
   d. He had been suspended from the football team for the rest of the season.

Izzy Multiple Choice Study/Quiz Questions page 2

7. In what state of mind is Marco right before he drives Izzy home?
    a. He is jealous of Tony.
    b. He is angry because Izzy will not go on another date with him.
    c. He is hopeful he can play football again.
    d. He is drunk and angry.

8. What two tragic events occur at the end of chapter two?
    a. Marco swerves off the road and into a tree. Half of Izzy's right leg is amputated.
    b. Marco gets in a fight with Tony. Izzy has to go to the hospital.
    c. Izzy's best friend drives drunk and hits another motorist.
    d. Marco forces Izzy to drive his VW, and she swerves off the road and crashes into a tree.

Izzy Multiple Choice Study/Quiz Questions page 3

<u>Chapters 3 and 4</u>
1. Who is little Izzy?
    a. Izzy's pet cat that wakes her up every morning
    b. Izzy, as nicknamed by her parents
    c. A miniaturized version of Izzy that Izzy pictures in her mind
    d. Izzy's cousin who is two years younger than Izzy

2. What school activity does Izzy miss?
    a. Math Club
    b. Latin Club
    c. Tennis
    d. Chorus

3. Who is Rosamunde Webber?
    a. Izzy's psychological nurse who talks with Izzy about school
    b. A smart girl at school who does not "fit in"
    c. Tony Marcel's girlfriend who was also at the party the night of Izzy's accident
    d. Izzy's doctor who has known Izzy since she was a baby

4. Why does Izzy's best friend, Suzy, call Izzy from the pay phone at school?
    a. She needs to explain Izzy's homework assignments.
    b. She tells Izzy how much everyone misses her at school.
    c. Suzy wants to tell Izzy that Marco is sorry and worried.
    d. Suzy calls from school so all of Izzy's friends can say hello too.

5. What is odd about the visit from Izzy's friends, Suzy, Lisa, and Lauren?
    a. They do not have anything to talk about.
    b. They do not have permission to be in Izzy's hospital room.
    c. They keep repeating the same things.
    d. They ask too many personal questions.

6. At the end of chapter four, what does Izzy look at?
    a. She looks over all her make-up assignments.
    b. She looks through all the items in the suitcase her mother brought.
    c. She looks at the photo of her cheerleading squad.
    d. She looks at what her friends had been staring at, her legs.

Izzy Multiple Choice Study/Quiz Questions page 4

Chapters 5 and 6

1. Right after Izzy realizes her leg has been amputated, who shows up and why?
    a. A nurse arrives to massage her legs.
    b. Suzy, Lauren, and Lisa arrive for a visit.
    c. Marco arrives to apologize.
    d. Her grandparents arrive to see how she's feeling.

2. Who has not sent Izzy a get-well card, or anything?
    a. Lisa
    b. Suzy
    c. Francie
    d. Marco

3. When Izzy wakes up in the darkness of the night, what does she do?
    a. Eat
    b. Watch television
    c. Cry
    d. Call her parents

4. Why does Izzy's brother, Jack, not visit her in the hospital?
    a. Joel implies Jack hasn't been feeling well.
    b. Joel implies that Jack is doing poorly in school, and he needs to study for some exams.
    c. Joel implies it's because of a girl.
    d. Jack is in Florida for fall break.

5. According to Dr. Epstein, how long will it be before Izzy can return home?
    a. "Not for six to eight weeks."
    b. "Not for at least three months."
    c. "Sometime between Thanksgiving and Christmas."
    d. "Not for at least a week more, and probably closer to two weeks."

6. Instead of telling her parents she is feeling depressed, what does Izzy tell her parents?
    a. She tells them she is scared.
    b. She tells them she is tired.
    c. She tells them she misses school.
    d. She tells them she is lonely.

7. What is Izzy's guess about why Suzy and Lisa visited?
    a. "Somebody had given them an earful," and "they'd been forced to come.'"
    b. "Suzy's mother probably drove them directly to the hospital."
    c. "My mother had called Suzy and asked her to stop by to cheer me up."
    d. "They were feeling guilty about not seeing me enough."

Izzy Multiple Choice Study/Quiz Questions page 5

<u>Chapters 7 and 8</u>
1. What question does everyone ask Izzy?
    a. When are you going home?
    b. How are you?
    c. Can you feel your leg?
    d. Was Marco driving the car?

2. What does Rosamunde Webber say when she first sees Izzy?
    a. "You look better than I expected."
    b. "Why did they put you in this dark room?"
    c. "Suzy asked me to drop off your assignments."
    d. "You look terrible."

3. Who does Izzy's mother see crying at the hospital?
    a. Dr. Epstein
    b. Rosamunde
    c. Lauren
    d. Lisa

4. What does Izzy ask Dr. Epstein?
    a. If she can get some better food.
    b. If she can stop the physical therapy.
    c. If she can watch when he changes the bandages on her leg.
    d. If he wants some more of her grandmother's homemade cookies.

5. Who does Dr. Epstein compare Izzy to and why?
    a. The character Dora in Dickens' *David Copperfield* because her eyes are so big
    b. Izzy's mother because Izzy has the same temperament as her mother
    c. His own daughter who is a few years older than Izzy
    d. A character from a silent movie because she is so quiet

6. How does Rosamunde respond to Izzy's telephone call from her brother Jack?
    a. Rosamunde laughs hysterically because Jack is telling Izzy jokes.
    b. Rosamunde starts to cry because Jack is upsetting Izzy.
    c. Rosamunde grabs the phone from Izzy, confronts Jack, and makes him hang up.
    d. Rosamunde listens carefully to their conversation because she has a crush on Jack.

Izzy Multiple Choice Study/Quiz Questions page 6

Chapters 9 and 10
1. What does Rosamunde hang on the hospital room wall?
    a. She hangs a floral needlepoint design that her mother made for Izzy.
    b. She hangs a batik cloth covered with animals that her mother made.
    c. She hangs a copy of the Latin Club's recruitment poster.
    d. She hangs the high school banner and a photograph of the cheerleading squad.

2. Where are Izzy's parents going dressed in their formal wear?
    a. They are going to a classical music concert.
    b. They are attending Mr. Lingard's Christmas party at the Country Club.
    c. They are attending a formal dinner dance.
    d. They are going to the hospital ball.

3. According to Rosamunde, what other meanings for "nice" are there?
    a. "sarcastic, like a smart remark or humorous form of expression"
    b. "fine, delicate, precise, like a nice distinction, or a nice point"
    c. "satisfied, like something done well"
    d. "refreshed in spirits, like a healthy person"

4. When Joel visited Izzy, why did he not allow Jack to come with him?
    a. Joel had been suspended from school.
    b. Joel had been very sick.
    c. Jack and Joel had been arguing.
    d. Joel was too angry.

5. What is the first thing Izzy wants to do when she gets home?
    a. She wants to watch television and sleep in her own bed.
    b. She wants to have her friends over for a welcome home dinner.
    c. She wants to put on normal clothes and listen to her albums.
    d. She wants to order a pizza with double cheese, sausage, green peppers and mushrooms.

6. Mrs. Lingard thinks Rosamunde must feel uncomfortable. Why?
    a. Mrs. Lingard thinks Rosamunde must feel uncomfortable because of the way Rosamunde looks.
    b. Mrs. Lingard thinks Rosamunde feels uncomfortable because Rosamunde is very shy.
    c. Mrs. Lingard thinks Rosamunde feels uncomfortable because they do not know each other.
    d. Mrs. Lingard thinks Rosamunde must feel uncomfortable because Rosamunde is lying about something.

Izzy Multiple Choice Study/Quiz Questions page 7

7. Rosamunde knows Izzy is lying about the details of the accident. Instead of lying about the accident, what does Rosamunde offer to tell her policeman father?
   a. "I can say you are scared about what will happen to Marco."
   b. "I can say you said you couldn't tell them anything more than you already have."
   c. "I can say you're confused about what to do."
   d. "I can say you are not prepared to talk until you get home."

8. When Izzy returns home, what has changed?
   a. The furniture has been rearranged to make it easier for Izzy to get around.
   b. So Izzy doesn't have to climb stairs, there's a new sleeper sofa in the downstairs den.
   c. The house seems too quiet and empty.
   d. Her parents' bedroom has been redecorated and is now Izzy's bedroom.

Izzy Multiple Choice Study/Quiz Questions page 8

Chapter 11 and 12

1. Prior to Izzy's return home, how had Francie often felt toward Izzy?
    a. She had been jealous of Izzy because Izzy was prettier and easy to get along with.
    b. She had been proud of Izzy and wanted to be just like her.
    c. She had felt that they were a lot alike because they shared similar interests.
    d. She had felt happy being sisters because Izzy had lots of friends.

2. What did Mrs. Lingard remove from Izzy's closet?
    a. She removed all Izzy's pants.
    b. She removed all of Izzy's right shoes.
    c. She removed Izzy's cheerleading sweaters.
    d. She removed Izzy's stuffed animals.

3. Izzy figures out that Suzy is wearing whose letter sweater?
    a. Tony's
    b. Marco's
    c. Joel's
    d. Billy's

4. Among Izzy's friends, who possesses "the strong personality?"
    a. Suzy
    b. Lisa
    c. Lauren
    d. Deborah

5. When Rosamunde stops by to pick up the things she'd loaned, what makes her laugh?
    a. Izzy's outfit makes her laugh because it does not match.
    b. Thinking about how Izzy's friends act at school makes her laugh.
    c. The line of left foot shoes in Izzy's closet makes Rosamunde laugh.
    d. The Lingard's daily dinner preparations make Rosamunde laugh.

6. According to Rosamunde, has Marco learned his lesson?
    a. Yes, she feels pity for him because he feels so guilty.
    b. No, Rosamunde thinks he is transferring to a prep school so he can continue to party.
    c. Yes, he is no longer drinking and is serious about changing his ways.
    d. No, Rosamunde thinks he can't even learn from experience.

7. Who annoys Mrs. Lingard by honking a car horn?
    a. Suzy
    b. Francie
    c. Mr. Webber
    d. Joel and Jack

Izzy Multiple Choice Study/Quiz Questions page 9

Chapters 13 and 14

1. What homework assignment does Izzy have trouble understanding?
   - a. She has trouble understanding the world history project requirements.
   - b. She has trouble with the geometry proofs.
   - c. She has trouble understanding what all the biology definitions mean.
   - d. She has trouble understanding English, specifically the play *Romeo and Juliet*.

2. Who does not return Izzy's telephone calls?
   - a. Suzy
   - b. Lisa
   - c. Lauren
   - d. Rosamunde

3. Who are fighting in the first scene of *Romeo and Juliet*?
   - a. Romeo and his servant are fighting.
   - b. The servants are fighting.
   - c. Romeo and Juliet are fighting.
   - d. Juliet and her nurse are fighting.

4. What makes Mrs. Jones, Izzy's physical therapy nurse, smile?
   - a. Izzy tells her a knock-knock joke.
   - b. Izzy tells her that she was thinking about *Romeo and Juliet*.
   - c. Izzy tells her about her attempts to cook.
   - d. Izzy tries to demonstrate one of her cheerleading moves.

5. Izzy does not want to get a hair cut. Why?
   - a. Izzy is not ready to face the public because people will stare at her.
   - b. Her mother wants it cut, but she likes it pulled back in a ponytail.
   - c. She thinks it will be too difficult to keep styled.
   - d. She has not made up her mind what style she wants.

6. How does Suzy describe Rosamunde?
   - a. Like a nerdy intellectual
   - b. A type of snobby know-it-all who thinks she's better than everyone else
   - c. A teacher's pet type
   - d. Sort of a leech who is definitely not cool

7. What game is the center of a boys versus girls competition?
   - a. Clue
   - b. Monopoly
   - c. Trivial Pursuit
   - d. Chess

Izzy Multiple Choice Study/Quiz Questions page 10

8. According to Joel, what does Jack underestimate in Izzy?
        a. He underestimates her persistence.
        b. He underestimates her forgiveness.
        c. He underestimates her brains.
        d. He underestimates her ability to get along with others.

Izzy Multiple Choice Study/Quiz Questions page 11

Chapters 15 - 17

1. Who pays Izzy an unexpected visit?
    a. Marco and Tony Marcel
    b. Dr. Epstein and Mrs. Jones
    c. Mr. and Mrs. Webber
    d. Tony Marcel and Deborah

2. Izzy has been asked to join what selective school activity?
    a. The Honor Society
    b. The school paper
    c. The gifted and talented art program
    d. The math team

3. What does Adelia suggest Izzy wear?
    a. Denim overalls
    b. Long skirts
    c. Trousers, pinned up in the back
    d. Multiple layers for outdoor exercise

4. What does Izzy want to borrow from Francie?
    a. Izzy wants to borrow Francie's colored pens.
    b. Izzy wants to borrow Francie's sweater.
    c. Izzy wants to borrow Francie's backpack.
    d. Izzy wants to borrow Francie's dictionary.

5. How does Izzy respond when Rosamunde asks, "What do you think of me?"
    a. Izzy responds, "I can't begin to describe you!"
    b. Izzy responds, "You're like a long-lost friend."
    c. Izzy responds, "You are definitely weird, but good weird."
    d. Izzy responds, "You are too smart for your own good."

6. Why is Mrs. Lingard a little concerned about Rosamunde?
    a. She is concerned because Rosamunde is teaching Izzy too much too soon, and she's worried Izzy will get hurt.
    b. She is concerned because Rosamunde is "not as outgoing as Izzy's other friends."
    c. She is concerned because Rosamunde is "so different, in everything, her attitudes, her background, her values."
    d. She is concerned because she has not met Rosamunde's parents.

Izzy Multiple Choice Study/Quiz Questions page 12

Chapters 18 and 19

1. What is Mr. Lingard thinking of putting in the backyard?
   a. A tennis court
   b. A sunken garden
   c. A tree that looks like the one Izzy is needlepointing
   d. A swimming pool

2. How does Izzy respond to Francie's complaint that Izzy gets everything just because she's crippled?
   a. She doesn't say anything back to Francie.
   b. She responds by saying, "Every cloud has a silver lining."
   c. She responds by saying, "I may be crippled, but I'm still Izzy."
   d. She leaves her family and goes to her bedroom.

3. What scares Izzy about her return to school?
   a. She's scared she will be unable to go up and down stairs.
   b. She is scared of facing all the people, especially Marco Griggers.
   c. She's scared of not having anyone to help her.
   d. She's scared of not having any friends to hang out with.

4. According to Rosamunde, why has Suzy "dropped" Marco Griggers?
   a. Suzy has realized that he was lying about the accident.
   b. Suzy has discovered that Marco is really selfish and arrogant.
   c. Suzy does not want to make Izzy feel bad when Izzy returns to school.
   d. Suzy has found someone better, a college boy.

5. What does Izzy tell Rosamunde and make her promise not to tell anyone?
   a. Izzy tells Rosamunde that she is often depressed and cries herself to sleep.
   b. Izzy tells Rosamunde that Suzy and Lauren no longer visit or call her.
   c. Izzy tells Rosamunde the truth about what happened the night of the accident.
   d. Izzy tells Rosamunde that she plans on transferring to a new school.

6. How does Rosamunde get Izzy to go to school?
   a. She shows up at Izzy's house on Thursday morning.
   b. She tells Izzy that Izzy will fail if she does not return.
   c. She promises Izzy she will get a haircut.
   d. She tells Izzy to think of her future goals, like college.

Izzy Multiple Choice Study/Quiz Questions page 13

Chapters 20-22

1. Excluding Izzy, how many people are on the school newspaper staff?
    a. 5
    b. 30
    c. 15
    d. 25

2. While at school, what makes Izzy cry?
    a. Her Latin teacher yells at her for being late.
    b. She sees the cheerleaders practicing their new routine.
    c. Someone quickly cuts past her, and she falls on her face.
    d. Lauren does not talk to her.

3. What does Izzy want to give Rosamunde for Christmas?
    a. Money, to purchase the game Trivial Pursuit
    b. A haircut
    c. A new jacket
    d. Movie tickets

4. How does Izzy spend New Year's Eve?
    a. She spends New Year's Eve watching rented movies.
    b. She spends New Year's Eve babysitting Francie.
    c. She spends New Year's Eve at Rosamunde's house.
    d. She spends New Year's Eve baking cookies.

5. At Lisa's party, how does Lauren act toward Izzy?
    a. When Lauren sees Izzy, she pretends that Izzy is her best friend again.
    b. Lauren acts like she is sick and has to go home.
    c. Lauren tries to tell Izzy she is sorry.
    d. When Izzy moves into the same room as Lauren, Lauren leaves.

6. What does Tony Marcel forget that causes "little Izzy" to do an impossible back flip?
    a. Tony forgets to remind Izzy about the newspaper deadline.
    b. Tony forgets to wait for Deborah.
    c. Tony forgets to tell Izzy her newspaper assignment for the day.
    d. Tony forgets to bring Izzy her crutches.

7. When Izzy sees Marco and Georgie Lowe together, what question does she ask Georgie?
    a. "Are you going to go out with him?"
    b. "Are you impressed because he is a senior?"
    c. "Don't you know you're better than him?"
    d. "Do you want to know the truth?"

ANSWER KEY - MULTIPLE CHOICE STUDY/QUIZ QUESTIONS
Izzy, Willy-Nilly

Chapters 1 and 2	Chapters 3 and 4	Chapters 5 and 6	Chapters 7 and 8
1. A	1. C	1. A	1. B
2. C	2. B	2. D	2. D
3. C	3. B	3. C	3. B
4. B	4. C	4. C	4. C
5. D	5. A	5. D	5. A
6. C	6. D	6. B	6. C
7. D		7. A	
8. A			

Chapters 9 and 10	Chapters 11 and 12	Chapters 13 and 14	Chapters 15-17
1. B	1. A	1. D	1. D
2. C	2. B	2. A	2. B
3. B	3. B	3. B	3. C
4. D	4. A	4. B	4. A
5. D	5. C	5. A	5. C
6. A	6. D	6. D	6. C
7. B	7. C	7. C	
8. D		8. C	

Chapters 18 and 19	Chapters 20-22
1. D	1. C
2. B	2. C
3. B	3. B
4. D	4. B
5. C	5. D
6. A	6. D
	7. A

PREREADING VOCABULARY WORKSHEETS

VOCABULARY CHAPTERS 1 and 2 *Izzy, Willy-Nilly*

Part I: Using Prior Knowledge and Contextual Clues
Below are the sentences in which the vocabulary words appear in the text. Read the sentence. Use any clues you can find in the sentence combined with your prior knowledge, and write what you think the underlined words mean on the lines provided.

1. Then he told me about <u>contusions</u> and bruising "of the upper torso," which he sounded pretty bored with.

_____

2. Multiple fracture of tibia and <u>fibula</u>, a closed fracture of the femur.

_____

3. I <u>avulsed</u> the debride tissue, tried to align the bones . . . .

_____

4. "We've got you <u>stabilized</u>," Dr. Carstairs told me, and we'll keep the leg pinned up."

_____

5. The leg may well have to be <u>amputated</u>.

_____

6. We can't predict how much tissue <u>necrosis</u> there will be, and that leads, of course, to the danger of infection.

_____

7. They've run a tube called a <u>catheter</u> directly up into your bladder.

_____

8. Dr. Epstein, my <u>pediatrician</u>, came into my room that morning.

_____

9. He was a <u>notorious</u> flirt, but I couldn't see what harm driving home with him would do.

_____

39

Izzy, Willy-Nilly Vocabulary Worksheet Chapters 1 and 2   Continued

Part II: Determining the Meaning
Match the vocabulary words to their dictionary definitions.

___ 1. contusions
___ 2. fibula
___ 3. avulsed
___ 4. stabilized
___ 5. amputated
___ 6. necrosis
___ 7. catheter
___ 8. pediatrician
___ 9. notorious

A. widely, but unfavorably known
B. the long, thin outer bone of the human leg, between the knee and the ankle
C. a medical specialist dealing with the development and care of infants and children
D. cut off (an arm, leg, etc.) by surgery
E. the death or decay of tissue in a part of the body
F. a tube inserted into the body used for draining urine from the bladder
G. kept from changing
H. bruises
I. tore away by surgical traction

VOCABULARY CHAPTERS 3 and 4 *Izzy, Willy-Nilly*

Part I: Using Prior Knowledge and Contextual Clues
Below are the sentences in which the vocabulary words appear in the text. Read the sentence. Use any clues you can find in the sentence combined with your prior knowledge, and write what you think the underlined words mean on the lines provided.

1. I'm old enough to know what that considering look means, when she's trying to be <u>objective</u> about one of her own children.

   _____

2. I knew that would bother her, because everyone thinks all girls ought to be <u>liberated</u> and everything.

   _____

3. A good mother travels prepared for any <u>contingency</u>.

   _____

4. It's okay Jane, it's standard practice after a <u>trauma</u>.

   _____

5. Look, if Hendrik had an account that barely escaped <u>bankruptcy</u> he'd watch it carefully for a while, wouldn't he?

   _____

6. She wasn't telling the truth; I could tell by the way she hesitated and said something <u>indefinite</u>.

   _____

7. I unwrapped the box and then took out a stuffed cat, made of something that felt like an <u>angora</u> sweater, made to be floppy and cuddly.

   _____

8. She's a <u>psychological</u> liaison nurse, whatever that means.

   _____

Izzy, Willy-Nilly Vocabulary Worksheet Chapters 3 and 4 Continued

Part II: Determining the Meaning
Match the vocabulary words to their dictionary definitions.

___ 1. objective
___ 2. liberated
___ 3. contingency
___ 4. trauma
___ 5. bankruptcy
___ 6. indefinite
___ 7. angora
___ 8. psychological

A. not precise or clear in meaning; vague
B. a possible, unforeseen, or accidental occurrence
C. the state of being unable to pay debts
D. of the mind; mental
E. without bias or prejudice
F. a soft yarn used for sweaters
G. a bodily injury, wound, or shock
H. set free; released

VOCABULARY CHAPTERS 5 and 6 *Izzy, Willy-Nilly*

Part I: Using Prior Knowledge and Contextual Clues
Below are the sentences in which the vocabulary words appear in the text. Read the sentence. Use any clues you can find in the sentence combined with your prior knowledge, and write what you think the underlined words mean on the lines provided.

1. You can't put a prosthetic device on tender skin.

   _____

2. The only edible thing on my breakfast tray was a piece of toast.

   _____

3. My mother came by and asked me why I hadn't started the needlepoint kit.

   _____

4. Joel is the cutest, but Jack has the best smile, and he's got a smoldering kind of personality.

   _____

5. It was so solitary there inside myself.

   _____

6. There I was, and this horrible thing has happened to me, and she was thinking that it was inconvenient to have me home.

   _____

7. This, I knew, was a way of looking for anemia.

   _____

8. My parents both came and played three-handed rummy and talked about one thing and another.

   _____

Izzy, Willy-Nilly Vocabulary Worksheet Chapters 5 and 6 Continued

Part II: Determining the Meaning
Match the vocabulary words to their dictionary definitions.

___ 1. prosthetic   A. an embroidery of threads upon a canvas
___ 2. edible   B. a condition in which there is a reduction of the number of
                             red blood corpuscles in the bloodstream, resulting in
                             paleness and weakness
___ 3. needlepoint   C. being alone
___ 4. smoldering   D. not favorable to one's comfort; difficult to do
___ 5. solitary   E. burning
___ 6. inconvenient   F. a replacement part of the body by an artificial substitute
___ 7. anemia   G. anything fit to be eaten
___ 8. rummy   H. a card game

VOCABULARY CHAPTERS 7 and 8 *Izzy, Willy-Nilly*

Part I: Using Prior Knowledge and Contextual Clues
Below are the sentences in which the vocabulary words appear in the text. Read the sentence. Use any clues you can find in the sentence combined with your prior knowledge, and write what you think the underlined words mean on the lines provided.

1. My grandmother Lingard sent me a <u>linzertorte</u>, cut into squares and packed into a cookie tin.

___

2. <u>Physical Therapy</u> it said on the door. PT. I didn't want to go in.

___

3. I've got this ache in my little finger joint on my left hand, which might be <u>juvenile</u> arthritis.

___

4. It's not that bad, not at all, considering. It's just <u>bland</u>.

___

5. I heard her <u>sarcasm</u>, but I didn't answer it.

___

6. Geez, this thing makes me feel <u>decrepit</u>, really decrepit.

___

7. "How's Francie?" I asked, which is always a good <u>diversionary</u> tactic.

___

8. She was glad I was crippled, I thought, because I was a <u>privileged</u> person, a white girl from a well-to-do background.

___

9. He sounded <u>certifiable</u>. He sounded like he was about to rip the whole phone off the wall.

___

Izzy, Willy-Nilly Vocabulary Worksheet Chapters 7 and 8 Continued

Part II: Determining the Meaning
Match the vocabulary words to their dictionary definitions.

___ 1. linzertorte
___ 2. physical therapy
___ 3. juvenile
___ 4. bland
___ 5. sarcasm
___ 6. decrepit
___ 7. diversionary
___ 8. privileged
___ 9. certifiable

A. serving to distract the attention
B. insane
C. characteristic of children
D. treatment of injury by physical means, like exercise, rather than with drugs
E. worn out by old age
F. a rich pastry made of almond dough and a raspberry jam filling
G. a taunting or cutting remark
H. having a right, advantage or favor that is withheld from certain others or all others
I. tasteless

VOCABULARY CHAPTERS 9 and 10 *Izzy, Willy-Nilly*

Part I: Using Prior Knowledge and Contextual Clues
Below are the sentences in which the vocabulary words appear in the text. Read the sentence. Use any clues you can find in the sentence combined with your prior knowledge, and write what you think the underlined words mean on the lines provided.

1. That's what worries me, about hurting your feelings, or something. <u>Inadvertently</u>.

_____

2. When she unfolded it, I could see greens, too, in the <u>batik</u>.

_____

3. Has the enthusiasm <u>dwindled</u>?

_____

4. Fresh from the oven, <u>Piroshkis</u>, I love them.

_____

5. But – you haven't begun to know the breadth of my <u>repertoire</u>.

_____

6. I guess I'd better neaten things up here a little too, or they'll <u>evict</u> you.

_____

7. She looked sort of <u>deflated</u>.

_____

8. Well, yes, it does, if that's why you've looked so <u>peaked</u>.

_____

9. It means you have to face up to peoples' <u>preconceptions</u> right away.

_____

10. I had served through, like an <u>indentured servant</u>.

_____

Izzy, Willy-Nilly   Vocabulary Worksheet Chapters 9 and 10 Continued

Part II: Determining the Meaning
Match the vocabulary words to their dictionary definitions.

___ 1. inadvertently
___ 2. batik
___ 3. dwindled
___ 4. Peroshkis
___ 5. repertoire
___ 6. evict
___ 7. deflated
___ 8. peaked
___ 9. preconceptions
___ 10. indentured servant

A. to remove a tenant by legal procedure
B. thin and weak as from illness
C. the special skills, techniques, etc. of a particular person
D. opinions formed in advance
E. small pastry turnovers with a filling
F. unintentionally
G. cloth decorated with dye – made by coating the sections not to be dyed with removable wax
H. diminished
I. made smaller or less important
J. one who was voluntarily or involuntarily committed to working for someone for a fixed number of years

VOCABULARY CHAPTERS 11 and 12 *Izzy, Willy-Nilly*

Part I: Using Prior Knowledge and Contextual Clues
Below are the sentences in which the vocabulary words appear in the text. Read the sentence. Use any clues you can find in the sentence combined with your prior knowledge, and write what you think the underlined words mean on the lines provided.

1. Lined up on it were my favorite shampoo and conditioner, the <u>glycerin</u> soap that's better for my skin, and a jar of bath beads.

___

2. "And they catch me if I'm reading late," she continued her catalogue of <u>woes</u>.

___

3. I was glad I didn't have her problems, her moods, and her <u>intensity</u>.

___

4. Lisa wanted to <u>divert</u> me from the topic of Lauren.

___

5. I couldn't break the <u>illusion</u> that we were all just like normal, which was possibly true as long as I didn't roll away from the table.

___

6. I stayed in the kitchen with my mother, who was <u>marinating</u> chicken to broil.

___

7. My mother talked on the phone and I played games of <u>solitaire</u>.

___

8. Unless he's just <u>boasting</u> to keep up his reputation as a drinking man, or showing everybody that he doesn't feel guilty by not changing the way he acts.

___

9. "Mom," I told her, from my place back at the kitchen table, "your class <u>prejudices</u> are showing."

___

Izzy, Willy-Nilly Vocabulary Worksheet Chapters 11 and 12 Continued

Part II: Determining the Meaning
Match the vocabulary words to their dictionary definitions

___ 1. glycerin   A. suspicion intolerance, or irrational hatred of other races, regions, occupations, etc.
___ 2. woes   B. a card game played by one person
___ 3. intensity   C. bragging
___ 4. divert   D. an odorless, colorless liquid used in skin lotion and other products
___ 5. illusion   E. great energy of emotion, thought, or activity
___ 6. marinating   F. soaking meat or fish in a mixture of spices, and/or oil, wine, vinegar etc. before cooking
___ 7. solitaire   G. great sorrows, miseries etc.
___ 8. boasting   H. to distract the attention of
___ 9. prejudices   I. a false perception of what one sees

VOCABULARY CHAPTERS   Chapters 13 and 14   *Izzy, Willy-Nilly*

Part I: Using Prior Knowledge and Contextual Clues
Below are the sentences in which the vocabulary words appear in the text. Read the sentence. Use any clues you can find in the sentence combined with your prior knowledge, and write what you think the underlined words mean on the lines provided.

1. I didn't understand my reluctance to call her.

_____

2. She was rather diminutive altogether.

_____

3. The next morning, maybe because I was still thinking about the stupidity of hating somebody because of the color of the livery they wore, ...

_____

4. "Do you do gymnastics?" Francie asked, with all the subtlety of a sledgehammer.

_____

5. You haven't even looked at the conjugations I did.

_____

6. "Now that you've settled my life," I groused.

_____

7. But Jack always underestimates Izzy's brains.

_____

8. You just idealize people, Jo; you're not realistic at all.

_____

Izzy, Willy-Nilly Vocabulary Worksheet Chapters 13 and 14 Continued

Part II: Determining the Meaning
Match the vocabulary words to their dictionary definitions

___ 1. reluctance
___ 2. diminutive
___ 3. livery
___ 4. subtlety
___ 5. conjugations
___ 6. groused
___ 7. underestimates
___ 8. idealize

A. a uniform worn by servants or those in some particular group or trade
B. the ability to be delicately suggestive
C. the inflectional forms of verbs
D. to regard as perfect or more nearly perfect than is true
E. unwillingness
F. sets too low of an estimate or judgment
G. grumbled
H. very small

VOCABULARY CHAPTERS   Chapters 15-17   *Izzy, Willy-Nilly*

Part I: Using Prior Knowledge and Contextual Clues
Below are the sentences in which the vocabulary words appear in the text. Read the sentence. Use any clues you can find in the sentence combined with your prior knowledge, and write what you think the underlined words mean on the lines provided.

1. "They say the winds may gust up to seventy," Deborah said. "That makes it almost a gale."

2. The twins left in such boisterous good humor that I knew they had been relieved by what they had seen in me.

3. Francie shook her head emphatically.

4. All I know is next I start on a Nautilus machine, which even Adelia says is hard work, and her idea of hard work is – more than I can imagine.

5. We have to polish up your domestic skills, or else what will you have to offer a potential husband?

6. Good, your mother gets real butter, we'll make a genoise, you can beat it sitting down.

7. If you had something with a kind of sheen to it, like floss or something, for some of these leaves –

8. I told her, to reassure her, if she wanted that reassurance.

Izzy, Willy-Nilly Vocabulary Worksheet Chapters 15-17 Continued

Part II: Determining the Meaning
Match the vocabulary words to their dictionary definitions

___ 1. gale
___ 2. boisterous
___ 3. emphatically
___ 4. Nautilus
___ 5. domestic
___ 6. genoise
___ 7. sheen
___ 8. reassurance

A. a rich, moist spongecake, often with a creamy filling between its layers
B. a strong wind
C. restored confidence
D. noisy and lively
E. trademark for weight-lifting equipment that varies the resistance of the weights in proportion to muscular strength
F. done with emphasis
G. shininess; brightness; luster
H. having to do with the home or housekeeping

VOCABULARY CHAPTERS 18 and 19 *Izzy, Willy-Nilly*

Part I: Using Prior Knowledge and Contextual Clues
Below are the sentences in which the vocabulary words appear in the text. Read the sentence. Use any clues you can find in the sentence combined with your prior knowledge, and write what you think the underlined words mean on the lines provided.

1. Nobody listened to my objections until I finally asked them please to lay off.

_____

2. "It would certainly be convenient," I said.

_____

3. "We can negotiate," I said. "I'll let you trade TV hours or something, if you want to. . . .

_____

4. She went wailing out of the room and I tried to finish the dishes by myself.

_____

5. She smiled at me. "Touche."

_____

6. Until they throw me out for incompetence.

_____

7. She knew my mother thought she was intruding, ...

_____

8. But my mother didn't know what Rosamunde was up to; she had sort of judged and condemned Rosamunde as a clinger, and she thought Rosamunde was being rude.

_____

Izzy, Willy-Nilly Vocabulary Worksheet Chapters 18 and 19 Continued

Part II: Determining the Meaning
Match the vocabulary words to their dictionary definitions

    ____ 1. objections   A. disapproved of strongly
    ____ 2. convenient   B. to bargain or discuss in order to reach agreement
    ____ 3. negotiate   C. forcing oneself upon others without being asked
    ____ 4. wailing   D. easy to do, use, or get to; easily accessible
    ____ 5. touché   E. reasons for disapproving or disliking
    ____ 6. incompetent   F. incapable; unskilled
    ____ 7. intruding   G. used to acknowledge a successful point in debate
    ____ 8. condemned   H. long, pitiful crying

VOCABULARY CHAPTERS 20-22 *Izzy, Willy-Nilly*

Part I: Using Prior Knowledge and Contextual Clues
Below are the sentences in which the vocabulary words appear in the text. Read the sentence. Use any clues you can find in the sentence combined with your prior knowledge, and write what you think the underlined words mean on the lines provided.

1. Rosamunde dismissed her as <u>shallow</u>.

___

2. "I never did think you had enough <u>vanity</u>," she said.

___

3. I was too tired, I didn't need this—<u>humiliation</u>, and I was sprawled there on the floor, flat on my face.

___

4. Who wants a male secretary? They wouldn't know how to <u>kowtow</u> properly.

___

5. Don't <u>antagonize</u> her, okay?

___

6. About how she wants her family to be, what a good mother does – even why she does all that charity work, kind of like some aristocrat with her <u>noblesse oblige</u>.

___

7. Suzy hung around for awhile, carrying on this <u>disjointed</u> whispered conversation.

___

8. Then, I would concentrate on other things as well, <u>irrelevant</u> things, like the idea of getting Rosamunde over for regular swimming, once our pool was built.

___

9. "I don't mean to interrupt anything," I said, <u>repressing</u> the anger I could feel burning from my stomach.

___

Izzy, Willy-Nilly Vocabulary Worksheet Chapters 20-22 Continued

Part II: Determining the Meaning
Match the vocabulary words to their dictionary definitions

___ 1. shallow
___ 2. vanity
___ 3. humiliation
___ 4. kowtow
___ 5. antagonize
___ 6. noblesse oblige
___ 7. disjointed
___ 8. irrelevant
___ 9. repressing

A. lacking depth of character; superficial
B. holding back
C. not pertinent; not relevant
D. excessively proud of oneself or one's qualities or possessions
E. to show respect by kneeling and touching the ground with the forehead
F. feeling hurt pride or dignity by being or seeming foolish
G. disconnected
H. to oppose; to struggle against
I. the inferred obligation of people of high social position to behave nobly or kindly toward others

VOCABULARY ANSWER KEY
Izzy, Willy-Nilly

Chapters 1 and 2	Chapters 3 and 4	Chapters 5 and 6	Chapters 7 and 8
1. H	1. E	1. F	1. F
2. B	2. H	2. G	2. D
3. I	3. B	3. A	3. C
4. G	4. G	4. E	4. I
5. D	5. C	5. C	5. G
6. E	6. A	6. D	6. E
7. F	7. F	7. B	7. A
8. C	8. D	8. H	8. H
9. A			9. B

Chapters 9 and 10	Chapters 11 and 12	Chapters 13 and 14	Chapters 15-17
1. F	1. D	1. E	1. B
2. G	2. G	2. H	2. D
3. H	3. E	3. A	3. F
4. E	4. H	4. B	4. E
5. C	5. I	5. C	5. H
6. A	6. F	6. G	6. A
7. I	7. B	7. F	7. G
8. B	8. C	8. D	8. C
9. D	9. A		
10. J			

Chapters 18 and 19	Chapters 20-22
1. E	1. A
2. D	2. D
3. B	3. F
4. H	4. E
5. G	5. H
6. F	6. I
7. C	7. G
8. A	8. C
	9. B

DAILY LESSONS

LESSON ONE

Objectives
    1. To introduce students to the book *Izzy, Willy-Nilly*
    2. To relate the book to students own lives
    3. To make students stop and think about what it means to have a disability

Activity 1 and Notes

    Is there someone in your school or community who has been affected by a drunk driver? If you don't know of anyone personally, contact your local MADD chapter to help with this introductory activity. Find a person or some people who are willing to come into your classroom to talk with your students about their experiences. Invite them to bring pictures. The point is to show students real, live people who have been affected by drunk drivers, and what it has meant in their lives. This, in an attempt to introduce students to *Izzy, Will-Nilly* but also to bring home to students the importance of not drinking and driving.

    Introduce your guests and give them the opportunity to share their experiences. Allow time for your students to ask questions or share their own experiences that might be relevant.

    Be sure to get the contact information (names & addresses) from your guests.

Activity 2

    If time remains after your speakers have made their presentations and your students have shared their experiences, students should jot down their impressions: things they heard that impressed them or touched them in some way, and their reactions to those things. If there is no time remaining, students should do this for homework.

LESSON TWO

<u>Objectives</u>
1. To appropriately thank the guests who took time to come into your classroom
2. To show students how to write a thank you note
3. To connect the introductory activity with the book
4. To distribute the materials students will need in this unit

Note: Bring envelopes and stamps to class or have students do so.

<u>Activity #1</u>
Tell students to look at the notes they made after the presentations in the last class period. Get several students to share their impressions and reactions. Explain that the book they are going to read is about a high school girl, Izzy, who has part of her leg amputated after being in a car accident caused by a drunk driver.

<u>Activity #2</u>
Discuss with students what it must be like to share one's tragic experiences with others, how their guests may have felt about coming and talking with the class, and why they would have done it. Develop the idea of appreciating the fact that the guests did come and share their experiences, leading into the next activity of writing thank you notes.

<u>Activity #3</u>
Explain to students how to write a thank you note: the obvious parts of the letter or note, but more importantly what goes into the body. The introductory paragraph should thank you and what for. The paragraph or paragraphs that follow should be an expression of what the presentation meant to the student. Having students look at the notes they made about their impressions and reactions will help them develop what to say that will make it a personal note, not just a "rubber stamp" thank you. Discuss through example things students might or could write in their thank you letters to the guests.

<u>Activity #4</u>
Give students time to write their thank you notes. Each student should write to one of the guests of the student's choice. Provide the guests' names and addresses for students to use. If you choose to "grade" this assignment or look at the letters before they go out, just have students put their notes and envelopes together, not sealed, and collect them. If you don't want to see the notes first, have students seal their envelopes and collect them for mailing.

<u>Activity #5</u>
While students are writing their letters, distribute the books and materials students will use in this unit. If students finish writing early, they may begin to look at the materials.

Study Guides Students should read the study guide questions for each reading assignment prior to beginning the reading assignment to get a feeling for what events and ideas are important in the section they are about to read. After reading the section, students will (as a class or individually) answer the questions to review the important events and ideas from that section of the book. Students should keep the study guides as study materials for the unit test.

Vocabulary Prior to each reading assignment, students will do vocabulary work related to the section of the book they are about to read. Following the completion of the reading of the book, there will be a vocabulary review of all the words used in the vocabulary assignments. Students should keep their vocabulary work as study materials for the unit test.

Reading Assignment Sheet You need to fill in the reading assignment sheet to let students know by when their reading has to be completed. You can either write the assignment sheet up on a side blackboard or bulletin board and leave it there for students to see each day, or you can "ditto" copies for each student to have. In either case, you should advise students to become very familiar with the reading assignments so they know what is expected of them.

Extra Activities Center The Unit Resource Materials portion of this LitPlan contains suggestions for an extra library of related books and articles in your classroom as well as crossword and word search puzzles. Make an extra activities center in your room where you will keep these materials for students to use. (Bring the books and articles in from the library and keep several copies of the puzzles on hand.) Explain to students that these materials are available for students to use when they finish reading assignments or other class work early.

Nonfiction Assignment Sheet Explain to students that they each are to read at least one non-fiction piece from the in-class library at some time during the unit. Students will fill out a nonfiction assignment sheet after completing the reading to help you (the teacher) evaluate their reading experiences and to help the students think about and evaluate their own reading experiences.

Books Each school has its own rules and regulations regarding student use of school books. Advise students of the procedures that are normal for your school.

LESSON THREE

Objectives
1. To show students how to use the materials relating to the unit
2. To acquaint students with the vocabulary for chapters 1-2
3. To preview chapters 1-2
4. To read chapters 1-2
5. To evaluate students' oral reading

Activity #1

If you didn't have the opportunity to distribute materials in the last class period, do it now. If you did, tell students to look at the materials you distributed, and discuss how the materials are to be used.

Activity #2

Read through the study questions with your students. Explain to them that they should read the questions prior to doing the reading of each assignment so they have some clues about what will be important in their reading.

Activity #3

Do the vocabulary worksheet for chapters 1-2 orally, together, as a class to show students how the worksheets are to be done. Explain that students will do one of these for each reading assignment in this unit.

Activity #4

Begin the reading of the book. Have your students read orally so you can evaluate their oral reading. An oral reading evaluation form follows, for your convenience. Duplicate the form and use one for each student.

If students do not finish reading chapters 1-2 in class, they should do so as homework.

ORAL READING EVALUATION *Izzy, Willy-Nilly*

Name _____ Class _____ Date _____

SKILL	EXCELLENT	GOOD	AVERAGE	FAIR	POOR
Fluency	5	4	3	2	1
Clarity	5	4	3	2	1
Audibility	5	4	3	2	1
Pronunciation	5	4	3	2	1
	5	4	3	2	1
	5	4	3	2	1

Total _____ Grade _____

Comments:

LESSON FOUR

Objectives
1. To review the main ideas and events from chapters 1-2
2. To preview and read chapters 3-4

Activity #1

Give students a few minutes to formulate answers for the study guide questions for chapters 1 and 2, and then discuss the answers to the questions in detail. Write the answers on the board or overhead transparency so students can have the correct answers for study purposes.

Notes:

Answering the study questions for each section can get boring if it is done the same way every time. You might consider varying the ways it is done throughout the unit. For example students could write the answers as independent work, formulate answers in small groups or pairs, formulate answers as a class, or answer the questions as a quiz. If answers are formulated in any way other than the whole class doing so orally, be sure to gather the class together to discuss the answers so all students do have the correct answers for study purposes.

It is a good practice in public speaking and leadership skills for individual students to take charge of leading the discussions of the study questions. Perhaps a different student or pairs/groups of students could go to the front of the class and lead the discussion each day that the study questions are discussed during this unit. Of course, the teacher should guide the discussion when appropriate and be sure to fill in any gaps the students leave.

Activity #2

Give students time to preview the study questions and do the vocabulary worksheet for chapters 3-4. Whether you discuss the vocabulary answers or simply make the answer key available on the board for students to check their own work after they have had ample time to complete it, just be sure that they do get the right answers for study purposes.

Activity #3

If you did not complete the oral reading evaluations in the last class meeting, continue them as students read chapters 3-4. If you did complete them, students may read silently or in pairs (taking turns reading to each other). This reading assignment should be completed prior to the next class meeting.

LESSON FIVE

Objectives
1. To review the main ideas and events of chapters 3-4
2. To preview the study questions & vocabulary for chapters 5-6
3. To discuss the idea and effects of peer pressure
4. To have students practice writing to persuade
5. To evaluate students' writing skills
6. To get students to think about the characters in more depth and to tie the book into real life

Activity #1

Have students formulate answers to the study questions for chapters 3-4 and discuss the answers, as directed in Lesson Four.

Activity #2

Ask students, "Who are Izzy's friends?" Make a list of students' responses on the board. Ask, "Who on this list, if anyone, is/are Izzy's TRUE friend(s)?" This should lead to a discussion about Izzy's relationship with each character mentioned, combined with a discussion of what a TRUE friend is. Somewhere in the discussion, bring up a question about the influence of peer pressure on Izzy and her "friends." What role does peer pressure play in the lives of Izzy and her friends? What role does peer pressure play in your students' lives? Get students to give specific examples of how peer pressure affects their lives, and whether that is a good or bad thing.

Activity #3

Distribute Writing Assignment #1, discuss the directions in detail, and give students ample time to complete the assignment. Tell students whether the assignment is due at the end of this class meeting or at another time. Collect it accordingly.

There is time in Lesson Ten for you to have writing conferences with students. Filling out a Writing Evaluation Form as you grade this writing assignment will give you a good basis for the writing conference.

Activity #4

If students finish the writing assignment early, they should do the prereading work (preview the study questions and do the vocabulary worksheet) for chapters 5-6. The prereading work should be done as homework if students do not finish it in class.

WRITING ASSIGNMENT #1 *Izzy, Willy-Nilly*
Writing To Persuade

PROMPT
Izzy's life has changed forever. In addition to facing the loss of her leg, she must also address the tragic details of the accident. To complicate matters, Izzy's best friend, Suzy, seems more concerned about Marco than Izzy. Your assignment is to write a letter to Izzy that either: persuades Izzy to tell the truth about the night of the accident **OR** convinces Izzy to remain silent.

PREWRITING
Since Izzy is your intended audience, brainstorm a list of ways to influence her. Think about Izzy's friends and family. If she tells the truth, how would they react to her? Would relationships change? How would she be treated at school? Specifically, what would happen to Marco and the others at the party?

What might happen as a result of not telling the truth? Would it prevent further complications in her life? Would the secret become too difficult to keep? Might she inadvertently hurt others?

DRAFTING
Begin your letter by stating your position in the first paragraph. The body of the letter should include reasons to support your position. The final paragraph/closing should restate your strongest persuasive points to leave a lasting impression.

PROOFREADING
When you finish the rough draft of your composition, ask a student who sits near you to read it. After reading your rough draft, he/she should tell you what he/she liked best about your work, which parts were difficult to understand, and ways in which your work could be improved. Reread your paper considering your critic's comments, and make the corrections you think are necessary. Ask your classmate what he/she thought of each of the characters/events you chose for your assignment. Do a final proofreading of your paper double-checking your grammar, spelling, organization, and the clarity of your ideas.

WRITING EVALUATION FORM *Izzy, Willy-Nilly*

Name_____ Date _____

Grade_____

Circle One For Each Item:

Grammar:	correct	errors noted on paper
Spelling:	correct	errors noted on paper
Punctuation:	correct	errors noted on paper
Legibility:	excellent	good fair poor
	excellent	good fair poor
	excellent	good fair poor

Strengths:

Ways To Improve:

LESSON SIX

<u>Objectives</u>
    1. To check the vocabulary work from chapters 5-6
    2. To read chapters 5-6
    3. To give students the opportunity to finish their writing assignments if they did not do so in the last class period

<u>Activity 1</u>
Tell students to look at their vocabulary worksheets for chapters 5-6. Have students exchange papers to correct. Briefly discuss the correct answers so students have the right ones to study from.

<u>Activity 2</u>
Students should use this class period to read chapters 5-6. If you have not completed the oral reading evaluations, do so today. If you have finished, students may read silently or in groups. This assignment should be completed as homework if not finished in class.

If you did not collect the writing assignments in the last class period, students should finish those and hand them in before doing the reading.

LESSON SEVEN

Objectives
1. To review the main ideas and evens from chapters 5-6
2. To introduce the unit project
3. To preview the study questions and vocabulary for chapters 7-8
4. To read chapters 7-8

Activity 1

Discuss the study questions for chapters 5-6 as directed in Lesson Four.

Activity 2

Talk with students for a few minutes. Tell them Izzy has a physical disability: part of her right leg has been amputated. Ask students what other kinds of physical disabilities people may have. What disabilities, if any, did your guest speakers in the introductory lesson have? Make a list of the physical disabilities from students' responses.

Tell students that in a few days (class periods) they will be a part of a class project in which they will explore many of these disabilities.

Activity 3

Have students look at their study questions and vocabulary worksheets for chapters 7-8. Preview the questions and do the vocabulary together as a class.

Activity 4

Students should use the remainder of the class period to read chapters 7-8. This reading assignment should be completed prior to the next class meeting.

LESSON EIGHT

Objectives
1. To review the main ideas and events from chapters 7-8
2. To preview the study questions and vocabulary for chapters 9-10
3. To let students experience what it is like to have a disability
4. To read chapters 9-10

Activity 1

Challenge students to live with a disability for one whole day. You may wish to issue a simple eye patch students can wear to simulate a vision disability. You could have students bandage their three middle fingers together on one hand, put an arm in a sling, use crutches, splint a finger–or whatever is appropriate without endangering your students unnecessarily. Do warn students that they should be cautious, be careful, as they attempt to live with their "disability." They don't HAVE to keep their disability for 24 hours, but they should try to maintain it as long as they can up to a full day so they can experience the inconvenience and frustration.

Activity 2

Discuss the answers to the study questions for chapters 7-8 as directed in Lesson Four.

Activity 3

Put students in small groups of three or four students to do the prereading work for chapters 9-10. After students have completed the work, briefly discuss the answers to the vocabulary worksheet.

Activity 4

Students should use the remainder of the class period to read chapters 9-10. This assignment should be completed prior to the next class meeting.

LESSON NINE

Objectives
1. To review the main ideas and events of chapters 9-10
2. To check students' knowledge of chapters 1-10
3. To discuss students' experiences with their disabilities
4. To preview the study questions and vocabulary for chapters 11-12
5. To read chapters 11-12

Activity 1
Distribute the quizzes for chapters 1-10. Give students ample time to complete them, then have students swap papers for grading. Discuss the answers as students grade the papers. Collect the quizzes for recording the grades.

Activity 2
Briefly discuss the answers to the study questions for chapters 9-10 just to be sure everyone has the correct answers for study purposes.

Activity 3
Tell students to take out a sheet of paper. On the paper they should write:
their name
the "disability" they had
how long they remained "disabled"
what the 2 most difficult things related to their disability were
whether they were treated differently by anyone because of the disability
at least 2 interesting or noteworthy experiences they had while they were disabled
at least 2 comments they have about their experience

NOTE: You might want to write the above list on the board so students have easy access to it.

Activity 4
Ask students to share their experiences with the class. Brainstorm a list of things that would have been helpful to students as they coped with their disabilities. Tell students that they will further explore these ideas over the next several class periods.

Activity 5
Tell students that they are to preview the study questions, do the vocabulary work, and read chapters 11-12 prior to the next class period. They may use the remainder of this class to begin the assignment.

MULTIPLE CHOICE QUIZ CHAPTERS 1-10 *Izzy, Willy-Nilly*

1. In what ways is Izzy considered nice?
    a. She is easy to get along with, fun to have around, and likes people.
    b. She is a peer counselor and math tutor at her school.
    c. She often baby sits for her parents and neighbors.
    d. She listens well to others and helps them with their problems.

2. Who is Marco Griggers?
    a. A comical television character
    b. A police officer
    c. A boy Izzy had been out with the night of the accident.
    d. A therapist

3. Why does Izzy's best friend, Suzy, call Izzy from the pay phone at school?
    a. She needs to explain Izzy's homework assignments.
    b. She tells Izzy how much everyone misses her at school.
    c. Suzy wants to tell Izzy that Marco is sorry and worried.
    d. Suzy calls from school so all of Izzy's friends can say hello too.

4. Who is little Izzy?
    a. Izzy's pet cat that wakes her up every morning.
    b. Izzy, as nicknamed by her parents.
    c. A miniaturized version of Izzy that Izzy pictures in her mind
    d. Izzy's cousin who is two years younger than Izzy.

5. What is odd about the visit from Izzy's friends, Suzy, Lisa, and Lauren?
    a. They do not have anything to talk about.
    b. They do not have permission to be in Izzy's hospital room.
    c. They keep repeating the same things.
    d. They ask too many personal questions.

6. Instead of telling her parents she is feeling depressed, what does Izzy tell her parents?
    a. She tells them she is scared.
    b. She tells them she is tired.
    c. She tells them she misses school.
    d. She tells them she is lonely.

7. How does Rosamunde respond to Izzy's telephone call from her brother Jack?
    a. Rosamunde laughs hysterically because Jack is telling Izzy jokes.
    b. Rosmunde starts to cry because Jack is upsetting Izzy.
    c. Rosamunde grabs the phone from Izzy, confronts Jack, and makes him hang up.
    d. Rosamunde listens carefully to their conversation because she has a crush on Jack.

8. What does Rosamunde hang on the hospital room wall?
    a. She hangs a floral needlepoint design that her mother made for Izzy.
    b. She hangs a batik cloth covered with animals that her mother made.
    c. She hangs a copy of the Latin Club's recruitment poster.
    d. She hangs the high school banner and a photograph of the cheerleading squad.

9. Mrs. Lingard thinks Rosamunde must feel uncomfortable. Why?
    a. Mrs. Lingard thinks Rosamunde must feel uncomfortable because of the way Rosamunde looks.
    b. Mrs. Lingard thinks Rosamunde feels uncomfortable because Rosamunde is very shy.
    c. Mrs. Lingard thinks Rosamunde feels uncomfortable because they do not know each other.
    d. Mrs. Lingard thinks Rosamunde must feel uncomfortable because Rosamunde is lying about something.

10. When Izzy returns home, what has changed?
    a. The furniture has been rearranged to make it easier for Izzy to get around.
    b. So Izzy doesn't have to climb stairs, there's a new sleeper sofa in the downstairs den.
    c. The house seems too quiet and empty.
    d. Her parents' bedroom has been redecorated and is now Izzy's bedroom.

MULTIPLE CHOICE QUIZ ANSWERS   CHAPTERS 1-10   *Izzy, Willy-Nilly*

1. A
2. C
3. C
4. C
5. A
6. B
7. C
8. B
9. A
10. D

SHORT ANSWER QUIZ   CHAPTERS 1-10   *Izzy, Willy-Nilly*

1. In what ways is Izzy considered nice?

2. Who is Marco Griggers?

3. Why does Izzy's best friend, Suzy, call Izzy from the pay phone at school?

4. Who is little Izzy?

5. What is odd about the hospital visit from Izzy's friends, Suzy, Lisa, and Lauren?

6. Instead of telling her parents she is feeling depressed, what does Izzy tell her parents?

7. How does Rosamunde respond to Izzy's telephone call from her brother Jack?

8. What does Rosamunde hang on the hospital room wall?

9. Mrs. Lingard thinks Rosamunde must feel uncomfortable. Why?

10. When Izzy returns home, what has changed?

SHORT ANSWER QUIZ ANSWERS   CHAPTERS 1-10   *Izzy, Willy-Nilly*

Note: Student short answer responses may vary. Accept reasonable answers based on class discussions.

1. In what ways is Izzy considered nice?
    Examples include: easy to get along with, fun to have around, did the work she was told to do, tried to make peace in quarrels, liked people etc.

2. Who is Marco Griggers?
    He is the boy Izzy had been out with the night of the accident. He drove Izzy home while intoxicated and crashed his car. Izzy lost her right leg as a result of the accident.

3. Why does Izzy's best friend, Suzy, call Izzy from the pay phone at school?
    Suzy wants to tell Izzy that Marco is sorry and worried. He hopes that Izzy won't try to get even with him because everyone at the party could get in trouble too.

4. Who is little Izzy?
    She is a miniaturized version of Izzy that Izzy envisions in her mind.

5. What is odd about the hospital visit from Izzy's friends, Suzy, Lisa, and Lauren?
    They do not have anything to talk about.

6. Instead of telling her parents she is feeling depressed, what does Izzy tell her parents?
    She tells them she is tired.

7. How does Rosamunde respond to Izzy's telephone call from her brother Jack?
    Rosamunde grabs the phone from Izzy, confronts Jack, and makes him hang up.

8. What does Rosamunde hang on the hospital room wall?
    She hangs a batik cloth covered with animals that her mother made.

9. Mrs. Lingard thinks Rosamunde must feel uncomfortable. Why?
    She thinks Rosamunde must feel uncomfortable because of the way Rosamunde looks. . . "With that nose, and hair? And her figure?"

10. When Izzy returns home, what has changed?
    Her parents' bedroom, located on the first floor, is now her bedroom.

LESSON TEN

Objectives
1. To review the main ideas and events of chapters 11-12
2. To familiarize students with the Disabilities Act Laws
3. To preview the study questions and do the vocabulary work for chapters 13-14
4. To read chapters 13-14

Activity 1
Discuss the answers to the study questions for chapters 11-12 as directed in Lesson Four.

Activity 2
Distribute copies of the Guide To Disability Rights Laws. This document is reprinted in its entirety in the Unit Resource Materials section of this manual. It may be reprinted without infringement of copyrights. If your school has a paper shortage, you might want to consider making transparencies of the document and looking at it with your students using the overhead projector.

Read through this document with your students at whatever level you think they will understand it. The point is to make them aware of the fact that there are laws that protect and attempt to help people in our country who have disabilities. It will also give them a good introduction to reading non-fiction, real-life, government documents. Make sure they know this is just a guide to the laws. The actual laws can be found at this web address:
http://www.usdoj.gov/crt/ada/pubs/ada.txt

Activity 3
Give students the remainder of the class period to preview the study questions, do the vocabulary work, and read chapters 13-14. This assignment should be completed prior to the next class meeting.

NOTE: While students are working on this assignment, call individual students to your desk for mini writing conferences based on the writing evaluations you did for writing assignment 1.

LESSON ELEVEN

Objectives
1. To review the main ideas and events from chapters 13-14
2. To increase students' awareness of the types of disabilities
3. To expose students to non-fiction related to *Izzy, Willy-Nilly*
4. To preview the study questions and do the prereading vocabulary for chapters 15-17
5. To read chapters 15-17

Activity 1
Discuss the answers to the study questions for chapters 13-14 as directed in Lesson Four.

Activity 2
Tell students that prior to the next class meeting they should preview the study questions, do the vocabulary worksheet for and read chapters 15-17. If students finish the research assignment in Activity 3 early, they should start on the assignment for chapters 15-17.

Activity 3
Tell students that Izzy faces many challenges as she comes to grips with the fact that she has lost part of her right leg and tries to adapt to life following the accident. Accidents are not the only causes of disabilities. Diseases can also disable people. We hear these diseases mentioned in the news or people talking about them, but what are they, really?

Assign one of the following diseases to each of your students. If you have more students than diseases, you may want to put students in pairs or small groups to work on this assignment.

cystic fibrosis
cerebral palsy
Crohn's disease
osteoporosis
glaucoma
lupus
fibromyalgia
rheumatoid arthritis
multiple sclerosis
obesity
lyme disease
diabetes
heart disease: specifically, stroke
Alzheimer's disease

Take students to your library or media center. Distribute the Disease Research Worksheets to your students. Explain to them that they are to complete the worksheet using at least two different sources. Sources can be from the internet, magazines articles, videos, interviews, or any other reliable sources.

DISEASE RESEARCH WORKSHEET
Izzy, Willy-Nilly

Disease _____

Student's Name _____

Source 1:

Source 2:

Definition of the Disease:

Symptoms of the Disease:

Causes of the Disease:

Cures/Treatments for the Disease:

About how many people does this disease affect?

What interesting facts or information did you come across in your research?

LESSON TWELVE

<u>Objectives</u>
1. To review the vocabulary, main ideas, and events for chapters 15-17
2. To share the information gathered in the last class meeting
3. To provide all students with a handbook guide to common diseases
4. To preview the study questions and do the vocabulary work for chapters 18-19
5. To read chapters 18-19

<u>Activity 1</u>
Discuss the answers to the vocabulary worksheet for chapters 15-17, and discuss the answers to the study questions as directed in Lesson Four.

<u>Activity 2</u>
Have each student give a short (1 minute) oral report about the disease he/she researched in the last class meeting. Collect the research worksheets, compile them, and run off enough copies for each student to have a handbook of common diseases for reference. Distribute them in the next class period, or as soon as you are able to get them compiled.

<u>Activity 3</u>
Preview the study questions and do the vocabulary work for chapters 18-19 orally, together as a class.

<u>Activity 4</u>
Give students the remainder of the class period to read chapters 18-19. Tell them that they must have the reading completed prior to your next class meeting.

LESSON THIRTEEN

Objectives
1. To review the main ideas and events from chapters 18-19
2. To investigate how disability-friendly your school is
3. To preview the study questions and do the vocabulary work for chapters 20-22
4. To read chapters 20-22

Activity 1
Discuss the study questions for chapters 18-19 as directed in Lesson Four.

Activity 2
Tell students that they have seen and experienced what it means to have a disability, learned about the Disabilities Act, studied diseases that cause disabilities, and have been reading the thoughts and seeing the adjustment process of someone recently disabled, Izzy. Talk with your students about what things in your school are disability-friendly and which things are not, including instructional methods, building facilities, transportation issues, school regulations, participation in extracurricular activities, etc. Have students take notes during the discussion, so they can practice this skill. You keep a list of notes, too, so you can offer your students' thoughts to the person at your school in charge of implementing things that make the school more disability friendly and so you can have a good set of notes to check your students' notes against.

Collect your students' notes for grading and/or comments.

Activity 3
Give students the remainder of the class period to preview the study questions, do the vocabulary work, and do the reading for chapters 20-22. This assignment should be completed prior to the next class period.

LESSON FOURTEEN

Objectives
1. To review the main ideas and events from chapters 20-22
2. To tie together the non-fiction work the students have done with the fictional story
3. To have students practice writing to inform
4. To evaluate students' writing skills
5. To evaluate students' understanding of the book

Activity 1
Discuss the answers to the study questions for chapters 20-22 as directed in Lesson Four.

Activity 2
Distribute Writing Assignment #2 and discuss the directions in detail. Give students ample time to complete the assignment, then collect it for grading. You may want to make another set of Writing Evaluation Forms to use when grading this assignment. There is time in Lesson Eighteen for another set of mini writing conferences.

LESSONS FIFTEEN AND SIXTEEN

Objectives
1. To answer higher-level comprehension questions including interpretation, critical analysis and personal response
2. To use a variety of thinking skills that add to the understanding of the novel
3. To discuss the answers to the questions

Activity #1
Choose the questions from the Extra Discussion Questions/Writing Assignments which seem most appropriate for your students. A class discussion of these questions is most effective if students have been given the opportunity to formulate answers to the questions prior to the discussion. To this end, you may either have all the students formulate answers to all the questions, divide your class into groups and assign one or more questions to each group, or you could assign one question to each student in your class. The option you choose will make a difference in the amount of class time needed for this activity. Also, review the significance of the selected quotations which appear on the unit tests.

NOTE: The use of graphic organizers may be helpful to students in preparing their answers. Encourage them to use any diagrams or graphics that they feel are necessary.

WRITING ASSIGNMENT #2   *Izzy, Willy-Nilly*
Writing To Inform

PROMPT

Izzy does not want to return to school. She worries about how others will respond to her and how she will cope with the daily challenges and demands of school. It would help if more people understood what she was going through. Since you know many of Izzy's innermost thoughts, your assignment is to write an informative article that informs others how they can help her succeed at school.

PREWRITING

Think about Izzy's character traits, such as courage, honesty and self-reliance. She also does not want others to pity her. How should her peers and teachers treat her? At what times might she require assistance? How could help be offered without compromising her independence? Offer suggestions for after school social situations too.

DRAFTING

Begin you paper with an introductory paragraph that explains the purpose of the article. Additional paragraphs should focus on the various ways to "help" Izzy during and after school. The final paragraph should summarize the main points.

PROOFREADING

When you finish the rough draft of your composition, ask a student who sits near you to read it. After reading your rough draft, he/she should tell you what he/she liked best about your work, which parts were difficult to understand, and ways in which your work could be improved. Reread your paper considering your critic's comments, and make the corrections you think are necessary. Ask your classmate what he/she thought of each of the characters/events you chose for your assignment. Do a final proofreading of your paper double-checking your grammar, spelling, organization, and the clarity of your ideas.

EXTRA WRITING ASSIGNMENTS/DISCUSSION QUESTIONS *Izzy, Willy-Nilly*

Interpretation
1. Why is the book entitled, *Izzy, Willy-Nilly*?
2. Explain the significance of "Little Izzy?"
3. Why does Izzy keep many of her feelings to herself?
4. Describe Izzy's relationship with her friends.
5. In what ways does Rosamunde help Izzy face reality?
6. Describe Izzy's relationship with her family.
7. Why is physical appearance so important to Izzy's mother?
8. What stereotypes appear in the book?
9. Why are there no punishments for Marco?
10. Provide examples of peer pressure from the book.
11. Describe Cynthia Voigt's writing style. How does that effect the story?
12. What are the main conflicts in the story?
13. Where is the high point (climax) of the story?
14. What is the setting of the story? Is it important to the story?

Critical
1. Compare and contrast Izzy's relationship with Rosamunde to her relationships with her "best friends."
2. What is the significance of Izzy's relationship to her physical therapist?
3. In what ways has Izzy become less judgmental of others?
4. How does Izzy change from the beginning of the book to the end of the book?
5. Why does Marco only date younger girls?
6. What does Rosamunde gain from Izzy's friendship?
7. Why are people uncomfortable being around Izzy?
8. Besides Izzy, what other character shows signs of courage and strength?

Critical/Personal Response
1. Could Izzy always "be herself" with her best friends? Can you?
2. Why is Izzy flattered to be asked out by Marco?
3. Do you think Izzy's parents should have told Izzy about her leg amputation? Why or why not?
4. Do you think Marco ever apologizes to Izzy? Why or why not?
5. How come Izzy never complains?
6. Who are Izzy's real friends?
7. How do Izzy's experiences and struggles make her a better person?
8. Why do many of Izzy's problems remain unresolved at the end of the book?

Personal Response
1. What was your reaction to the book?
2. In what ways have the pressures of high school changed?
3. How realistic was the book's depiction of high school life?
4. What difficult situations have you faced?

QUOTATIONS *Izzy, Willy-Nilly*

1. "When bad news comes, you don't believe it right away. Not really. Or anyway, I didn't." Chapter 1

2. "I'd rather stay, but – I'll be no use to anyone if I don't get some sleep. A good mother would stay." Chapter 1

3. "And there I was, almost with two seniors fighting over me. I remember thinking that and reminding myself that neither one of them was really thinking about me at all." Chapter 2

4. "We don't cry, not the Lingards." Chapter 5

5. "What's a nice girl like you doing in a place like this?" Chapter 7

6. "Crying is like – a pressure valve on a radiator. You've got to let off pressure sometimes." Chapter 8

7. "It was just that whenever I was alone my mind slipped down into grayness and I couldn't stop it." Chapter 13

8. "It was the richness of it, the richness in me; there was so much more than before. Better too, I had to admit it, although if I could have gone back and changed things I wouldn't have hesitated for one minute to do that." Chapter 22

LESSON SEVENTEEN

Objective
To pull together and review all the vocabulary words covered in the unit

Activity
Choose one (or more) of the vocabulary review activities listed below and spend your class period as directed in the activity. Some of the materials for these review activities are located in the Vocabulary Resource Materials section of this manual.

VOCABULARY REVIEW ACTIVITIES

1. Divide your class into two teams and have an old-fashioned spelling or definition bee.

2. Give each of your students (or students in groups of two, three or four) an *Izzy, Willy-Nilly* Vocabulary Word Search Puzzle. The person (group) to find all of the vocabulary words in the puzzle first wins.

3. Give students an *Izzy, Willy-Nilly* Vocabulary Word Search Puzzle without the word list. The person or group to find the most vocabulary words in the puzzle wins.

4. Use an *Izzy, Willy-Nilly* Vocabulary Crossword Puzzle. Put the puzzle onto a transparency on the overhead projector (so everyone can see it), and do the puzzle together as a class.

5. Give students an *Izzy, Willy-Nilly* Vocabulary Matching Worksheet to do.

6. Divide your class into two teams. Use *Izzy, Willy-Nilly* vocabulary words with their letters jumbled as a word list. Student 1 from Team A faces off against Student 1 from Team B. You write the first jumbled word on the board. The first student (1A or 1B) to unscramble the word wins the chance for his/her team to score points. If 1A wins the jumble, go to student 2A and give him/her a definition. He/she must give you the correct spelling of the vocabulary word which fits that definition. If he/she does, Team A scores a point, and you give student 3A a definition for which you expect a correctly spelled matching vocabulary word. Continue giving Team A definitions until some team member makes an incorrect response. An incorrect response sends the game back to the jumbled-word face off, this time with students 2A and 2B. Instead of repeating giving definitions to the first few students of each team, continue with the student after the one who gave the last incorrect response on the team. For example, if Team B wins the jumbled-word face-off, and student 5B gave the last incorrect answer for Team B, you would start this round of definition questions with student 6B, and so on. The team with the most points wins!

7. Have students write a story in which they correctly use as many vocabulary words as possible. Have students read their compositions orally! Post the most original compositions on your bulletin board!

LESSON EIGHTEEN

Objectives
    1. To assess students' knowledge of the characters in the novel
    2. To have students practice writing their personal opinions
    3. To evaluate students' writing skills
    4. To bring the unit to a conclusion

Activity
    Distribute Writing Assignment #3, discuss the directions in detail, give students ample time to complete it, then collect the assignment for grading.

NOTE: While students are working on this assignment it would be a good time to have another set of mini writing conferences based on Writing Assignment #2.

LESSON NINETEEN

Objective
    To review the main ideas and events presented in the book

Activity
    Choose one of the review games/activities suggested in this unit and spend your class time as directed there.

WRITING ASSIGNMENT #3 *Izzy, Willy-Nilly*
Writing Personal Opinions

PROMPT

Many issues remain unanswered at the conclusion of *Izzy, Willy-Nilly*. While "little Izzy" is taking a step forward, there's much left open to speculation. Your task is to continue the book by writing about what happens in the future to Izzy, Rosamunde, Marco and one other character of your choice.

PREWRITING

Think about each character and their individual personality traits, experiences, and relationships. Have they changed since the conclusion of the book? If yes, how have they changed? What experiences have they had? What have they learned? What does their future hold?

DRAFTING

Begin you paper with an introductory paragraph that describes how much time has passed and reacquaints your audience with the characters. Subsequent paragraphs should focus on the accounts of individual characters. The final paragraph should restate your thoughts regarding the characters' futures.

PROOFREADING

When you finish the rough draft of your composition, ask a student who sits near you to read it. After reading your rough draft, he/she should tell you what he/she liked best about your work, which parts were difficult to understand, and ways in which your work could be improved. Reread your paper considering your critic's comments, and make the corrections you think are necessary. Ask your classmate what he/she thought of each of the characters/events you chose for your assignment. Do a final proofreading of your paper double-checking your grammar, spelling, organization, and the clarity of your ideas.

REVIEW GAMES/ACTIVITIES *Izzy, Willy-Nilly*

1. Ask the class to make up a unit test for *Izzy, Willy-Nilly*. The test should have 4 sections: matching, true/false, short answer, and essay. Students may use 1/2 period to make the test and then swap papers and use the other 1/2 class period to take a test a classmate has devised. (open book) You may want to use the unit test included in this packet or take questions from the students' unit tests to formulate your own test.

2. Take 1/2 period for students to make up true and false questions (including the answers). Collect the papers and divide the class into two teams. Draw a big tic-tac-toe board on the chalk board. Make one team X and one team O. Ask questions to each side, giving each student one turn. If the question is answered correctly, that students' team's letter (X or O) is placed in the box. If the answer is incorrect, no letter is placed in the box. The object is to get three in a row like tic-tac-toe. You may want to keep track of the number of games won for each team.

3. Take 1/2 period for students to make up questions (true/false and short answer). Collect the questions. Divide the class into two teams. You'll alternate asking questions to individual members of teams A & B (like in a spelling bee). The question keeps going from A to B until it is correctly answered, then a new question is asked. A correct answer does not allow the team to get another question. Correct answers are +2 points; incorrect answers are -1 point.

4. Have students pair up and quiz each other from their study guides and class notes.

5. Give students an *Izzy, Willy-Nilly* crossword puzzle to complete.

6. Divide your class into two teams. Use *Izzy, Willy-Nilly* crossword words with their letters jumbled as a word list. Student 1 from Team A faces off against Student 1 from Team B. You write the first jumbled word on the board. The first student (1A or 1B) to unscramble the word wins the chance for his/her team to score points. If 1A wins the jumble, go to student 2A and give him/her a clue. He/she must give you the correct word which matches that clue. If he/she does, Team A scores a point, and you give student 3A a clue for which you expect another correct response. Continue giving Team A clues until some team member makes an incorrect response. An incorrect response sends the game back to the jumbled-word face off, this time with students 2A and 2B. Instead of repeating giving clues to the first few students of each team, continue with the student after the one who gave the last incorrect response on the team. For example, if Team B wins the jumbled-word face-off, and student 5B gave the last incorrect answer for Team B, you would start this round of clue questions with student 6B, and so on. The team with the most points wins!

Review Games Page 2

8. Play What's My Line?. This is similar to the old television show. Students assume the roles of different characters from the epic. One student gives clues to the class, or to a panel of contestants. The contestants try to guess the identity of the guest. Students may enjoy assisting you in creating rules and procedures for the game.

9. Play Jeopardy. Divide the class into two groups. Assign each group a category or book from the epic and have them devise answers for that category. Play the game according to the television show procedures.

10. Play Drawing in the Details. This is similar to Pictionary. Divide students into teams. A student from one team draws a scene from the epic. (You may want to specify the Book or section.) Drawings should be kept simple, to keep the pace lively. Students in the opposing team locate the scene in their books and read it aloud. If they are incorrect, the illustrator's team has a chance to guess. Involve students in setting up a scoring system and any other necessary rules.

UNIT TESTS

SHORT ANSWER UNIT TEST 1 *Izzy, Willy-Nilly*

I. Short Answer

1. In what ways is Izzy considered nice?

2. Who is little Izzy?

3. Who did Dr. Epstein compare Izzy to and why?

4. When Izzy returns home, what has changed?

5. According to Rosamunde, has Marco learned his lesson?

6. Izzy did not want to get a haircut. Why?

7. Why is Izzy's mother a little concerned about Rosamunde?

8. What scares Izzy about her return to school?

9. At Lisa's party, how does Lauren act toward Izzy?

SHORT ANSWER UNIT TEST 1 *Izzy, Willy-Nilly* Page 2

II. Quotations. Explain the importance or significance of each of the following quotations.

1. "When bad news comes, you don't believe it right away. Not really. Or anyway, I didn't." (Chapter 1)

2. "And there I was, almost with two seniors fighting over me. I remember thinking that and reminding myself that neither one of them was really thinking about me at all." (Chapter 2)

3. "What's a nice girl like you doing in a place like this?" (Chapter 7)

4. "Crying is like – a pressure valve on a radiator. You've got to let off pressure sometimes." (Chapter 8)

5. "It was the richness of it, the richness in me; there was so much more than before. Better too, I had to admit it, although if I could have gone back and changed things I wouldn't have hesitated for one minute to do that." (Chapter 22)

SHORT ANSWER UNIT TEST 1 *Izzy, Willy-Nilly* Page 3

III. Essay

Describe Izzy's relationship with Rosamunde, how it develops during the course of the book, and its significance in relationship to the themes of the novel.

SHORT ANSWER UNIT TEST 1 *Izzy, Willy-Nilly* Page 4

IV. Vocabulary
Listen to the vocabulary words, and write them down. Then go back and write down the definition for each word.

1.

2.

3.

4.

5.

6.

7.

8.

9.

10.

ANSWER KEY SHORT ANSWER TEST 1 Izzy, Willy-Nilly

I. Short Answer

1. In what ways is Izzy considered nice?
    Examples include: easy to get along with, fun to have around, did the work she was told to do, tried to make peace in quarrels, liked people etc.

2. Who is little Izzy?
    She is a miniaturized version of Izzy that Izzy envisions in her mind.

3. What book character does Dr. Epstein compare Izzy to and why?
    He compares Izzy to the character Dora in Dickens' *David Copperfield* because Izzy's eyes are so big. Later in the book, Rosamunde reads aloud a passage from *David Copperfield*. At that time, Rosamunde mentions that Dora was "essentially a really nice person."

4. When Izzy returns home, what has changed?
    Her parents' bedroom, located on the first floor, is now her bedroom.

5. According to Rosamunde, has Marco learned his lesson?
    No, Rosamunde thinks he can't even learn from experience. "Unless he's lying, he's still driving around more drunk than he should be."

6. Izzy did not want to get a haircut. Why?
    Izzy is not ready to face the public because people will stare at her.

7. Why is Izzy's mother a little concerned about Rosamunde?
    Mrs. Lingard thinks Rosamunde is not Izzy's kind of friend because Rosamunde is " so different, in everything, her attitudes, her background, her values." She also thinks Rosamunde is a "clinger."

8. What scares Izzy about her return to school?
    She is scared of facing everyone, especially Marco Griggers.

9. At Lisa's party, how does Lauren act toward Izzy?
    When Izzy moves into the same room as Lauren, Lauren leaves.

ANSWER KEY SHORT ANSWER TEST 1– Izzy, Willy-Nilly

II. Quotations: Explain the importance or significance of each of the following quotations.

ANSWERS WILL VARY DEPENDING ON YOUR CLASS DISCUSSIONS AND THE LEVEL OF YOUR CLASS.

III. Essay
Describe Izzy's relationship with Rosamunde and how it develops through the course of the book.

ANSWERS WILL VARY DEPENDING ON YOUR CLASS DISCUSSIONS AND THE LEVEL OF YOUR CLASS.

IV. Vocabulary
Choose 10 of the vocabulary words. Read them orally for students to write down.

SHORT ANSWER UNIT TEST 2 *Izzy, Willy-Nilly*

I. Short Answer

1. Why did Izzy's parents not want her to go out with Marco?

2. Why does Izzy's best friend, Suzy, call Izzy from the pay phone at school?

3. Why is Izzy's mother a little concerned about Rosamunde?

4. According to Rosamunde, has Marco learned his lesson?

5. What does Izzy tell Rosamunde and make her promise not to tell anyone?

6. While at school, what makes Izzy cry?

7. When Izzy sees Marco and Georgia Lowe together, what question does she ask Georgie?

SHORT ANSWER UNIT TEST 2 – Izzy, Willy-Nilly Page 2

II. Quotations. Explain the importance or significance of each of the following quotations.

1. "I'd rather stay, but – I'll be no use to anyone if I don't get some sleep. A good mother would stay." (Chapter 1)

2. "And there I was, almost with two seniors fighting over me. I remember thinking that and reminding myself that neither one of them was really thinking about me at all." (Chapter 2)

3. "We don't cry, not the Lingards." (Chapter 5)

4. "What's a nice girl like you doing in a place like this?" (Chapter 7)

5. "It was just that whenever I was alone my mind slipped down into grayness and I couldn't stop it." (Chapter 13)

6. "It was the richness of it, the richness in me; there was so much more than before. Better too, I had to admit it, although if I could have gone back and changed things I wouldn't have hesitated for one minute to do that." (Chapter 22)

SHORT ANSWER UNIT TEST 2 *Izzy, Willy-Nilly* Page 3

III. Essay
At the conclusion of the book, what does Izzy learn about herself? Additionally, what does she learn about others?

SHORT ANSWER UNIT TEST 2 *Izzy, Willy-Nilly* Page 4

IV. Vocabulary
Listen to the vocabulary words, and write them down. Then go back and write down the definition for each word.

1.

2.

3.

4.

5.

6.

7.

8.

9.

10.

ANSWER KEY SHORT ANSWER TEST 2 *Izzy, Willy-Nilly*

I. Short Answer

1. Why did Izzy's parents not want her to go out with Marco?
    They did not know him. He hadn't been a friend of the twins'. Most of the other kids at the party would be older.

2. Why does Izzy's best friend, Suzy, call Izzy from the pay phone at school?
    Suzy wants to tell Izzy that Marco is sorry and worried. He hopes that Izzy won't try to get even with him because everyone at the party could get in trouble too.

3. Why is Mrs. Lingard a little concerned about Rosamunde?
    Mrs. Lingard thinks Rosamunde is not Izzy's kind of friend because Rosamunde is " so different, in everything, her attitudes, her background, her values." She also thinks Rosamunde is a "clinger."

4. According to Rosamunde, has Marco learned his lesson?
    No, Rosamunde thinks he can't even learn from experience. "Unless he's lying, he's still driving around more drunk than he should be."

5. What does Izzy tell Rosamunde and make her promise not to tell anyone?
    Izzy tells Rosamunde the truth about what happened the night of the accident.

6. While at school, what makes Izzy cry?
    Someone quickly cuts past her, and she falls on her face.
    Feeling humiliated, she waits until everyone is gone, except Rosamunde, and wails.

7. When Izzy sees Marco and Georgie Lowe together, what question does she ask Georgie?
    "Are you going to go out with him?"

ANSWER KEY SHORT ANSWER TEST 2 *Izzy, Willy-Nilly*

II. Quotations: Explain the importance or significance of each of the following quotations.

ANSWERS WILL VARY DEPENDING ON YOUR CLASS DISCUSSIONS AND THE LEVEL OF YOUR CLASS.

III. Essay
At the conclusion of the book, what does Izzy learn about herself? In addition to what she learns about herself, what does she learn about others?

ANSWERS WILL VARY DEPENDING ON YOUR CLASS DISCUSSIONS AND THE LEVEL OF YOUR CLASS.

IV. Vocabulary
Choose 10 of the vocabulary words. Read them orally for students to write down.

ADVANCED SHORT ANSWER UNIT TEST *Izzy, Willy-Nilly*

1. In what ways does Rosamunde help Izzy face reality?

2. What stereotypes appear in the book?

3. In what ways has Izzy become less judgmental of others?

4. Why are people uncomfortable being around Izzy?

5. How come Izzy never complains?

6. Why do many of Izzy's problems remain unresolved at the end of the book?

7. Do you think high school pressures have changed today? Why or why not?

ADVANCED SHORT ANSWER UNIT TEST Izzy, Willy-Nilly Page 2

II. Quotations. Explain the importance or significance of each of the following quotations.

1. "When bad news comes, you don't believe it right away. Not really. Or anyway, I didn't." (Chapter 1)

2. "And there I was, almost with two seniors fighting over me. I remember thinking that and reminding myself that neither one of them was really thinking about me at all." (Chapter 2)

3. "What's a nice girl like you doing in a place like this?" (Chapter 7)

4. "Crying is like – a pressure valve on a radiator. You've got to let off pressure sometimes." (Chapter 8)

5. "It was just that whenever I was alone my mind slipped down into grayness and I couldn't stop it." (Chapter 13)

6. "It was the richness of it, the richness in me; there was so much more than before. Better too, I had to admit it, although if I could have gone back and changed things I wouldn't have hesitated for one minute to do that." (Chapter 22)

ADVANCED SHORT ANSWER UNIT TEST *Izzy, Willy-Nilly* Page 3

III. Essay
Compare and contrast your school experiences to the school experiences of characters in the book. Include examples of peer/school pressures today as compared to the pressures depicted in the book.

ADVANCED SHORT ANSWER UNIT TEST *Izzy, Willy-Nilly* Page 4

IV. Vocabulary
Listen to the vocabulary words, and write them down. Then go back and write down the definition for each word.

1.

2.

3.

4.

5.

6.

7.

8.

9.

10.

MULTIPLE CHOICE UNIT TEST 1 *Izzy, Willy-Nilly*

I. Matching Unit Words. Write the letter of the correct description next to each unit word.

____ 1. Francie   A. What Lingards don't do

____ 2. Lauren   B. Francie often feels this way

____ 3. Depressed   C. Suzy thinks Rosamunde is _____.

____ 4. Ms. Hughes-Pincke   D. What Rosamunde hangs on the hospital wall

____ 5. Treasure Trove   E. Izzy's sister

____ 6. Cheerleader   F. Izzy's lower right leg was _____.

____ 7. Deborah   G. Izzy becomes part of this group

____ 8. Dr. Epstein   H. Izzy's twin brothers

____ 9. A batik cloth   I. Mrs. Lingard removes these from Izzy's closet

____ 10. Marco   J. Izzy envies Georgie's _____.

____ 11. Joel and Jack   K. Izzy's pediatrician

____ 12. The school paper staff   L. A friend who avoids Izzy

____ 13. Shoes   M. Izzy's psychological liaison nurse

____ 14. Dora   N. A character from David Copperfield

____ 15. Cry   O. Izzy often feels this way

____ 16. Amputated   P. After drinking heavily, he drove Izzy home

____ 17. Nice   Q. A place to purchase handmade crafts

____ 18. Jealous   R. Tony's girlfriend

____ 19. Not Cool   S. Izzy was a _____.

____ 20. Perfection   T. An adjective that describes Izzy

MULTIPLE CHOICE UNIT TEST 1 *Izzy, Willy-Nilly* Page 2

II. Multiple Choice.

1. In what ways is Izzy considered nice?
    a. She is easy to get along with, fun to have around, and likes people.
    b. She is a peer counselor and math tutor at her school.
    c. She often baby sits for her parents and neighbors.
    d. She listens well to others and helps them with their problems.

2. Who is little Izzy?
    a. Izzy's pet cat that wakes her up every morning
    b. Izzy, as nicknamed by her parents
    c. A miniaturized version of Izzy that Izzy pictures in her mind
    d. Izzy's cousin who is two years younger than Izzy

3. Who does Dr. Epstein compare Izzy to and why?
    a. The character Dora in Dickens' *David Copperfield* because her eyes are so big
    b. Izzy's mother because Izzy has the same temperament as her mother
    c. His own daughter who is a few years older than Izzy
    d. A character from a silent movie because she is so quiet

4. When Izzy returns home, what has changed?
    a. The furniture has been rearranged to make it easier for Izzy to get around.
    b. So Izzy doesn't have to climb stairs, there's a new sleeper sofa in the downstairs den.
    c. The house seems too quiet and empty.
    d. Her parents' bedroom has been redecorated and is now Izzy's bedroom.

5. According to Rosamunde, has Marco learned his lesson?
    a. Yes, she feels pity for him because he feels so guilty.
    b. No, Rosamunde thinks he is transferring to a prep school so he can continue to party.
    c. Yes, he is no longer drinking and is serious about changing his ways.
    d. No, Rosamunde thinks he can't even learn from experience.

6. Izzy does not want to get a hair cut. Why?
    a. Izzy is not ready to face the public because people will stare at her.
    b. Her mother wants it cut, but she likes it pulled back in a ponytail.
    c. She thinks it will be too difficult to keep styled.
    d. She has not made up her mind what style she wants.

MULTIPLE CHOICE UNIT TEST 1 *Izzy, Willy-Nilly* Page 3

Matching (cont.)

7. Why is Izzy's mother a little concerned about Rosamunde?
    a. She is concerned because Rosamunde is teaching Izzy too much too soon, and she's worried Izzy will get hurt.
    b. She is concerned because Rosamunde is "not as outgoing as Izzy's other friends."
    c. She is concerned because Rosamunde is "so different, in everything, her attitudes, her background, her values."
    d. She is concerned because she has not met Rosamunde's parents.

8. What scares Izzy about her return to school?
    a. She's scared she will be unable to go up and down stairs.
    b. She is scared of facing all the people, especially Marco Griggers.
    c. She's scared of not having anyone to help her.
    d. She's scared of not having any friends to hang out with.

9. At Lisa's party, how does Lauren act toward Izzy?
    a. When Lauren sees Izzy, she pretends that Izzy is her best friend again.
    b. Lauren acts like she is sick and has to go home.
    c. Lauren tries to tell Izzy she is sorry.
    d. When Izzy moves into the same room as Lauren, Lauren leaves.

10. What does Izzy tell Rosamunde and make her promise not to tell anyone?
    a. Izzy tells Rosamunde that she is often depressed and cries herself to sleep.
    b. Izzy tells Rosamunde that Suzy and Lauren no longer visit or call her.
    c. Izzy tells Rosamunde the truth about what happened the night of the accident.
    d. Izzy tells Rosamunde that she plans on transferring to a new school.

MULTIPLE CHOICE UNIT TEST 1 *Izzy, Willy-Nilly* Page 4

III. Vocabulary: Match the vocabulary words to their dictionary definitions.

_____ 1. Certifiable   A. Characteristic of children

_____ 2. Stabilized   B. Cut off (an arm, leg, etc.) by surgery

_____ 3. Angora   C. Bruises

_____ 4. Indefinite   D. Set free; released

_____ 5. Edible   E. A bodily injury, wound, or shock

_____ 6. Smoldering   F. The state of being unable to pay debts

_____ 7. Rummy   G. Kept from changing

_____ 8. Juvenile   H. Insane

_____ 9. Amputated   I. Not precise or clear in meaning

_____ 10. Contusions   J. A soft yarn used for sweaters

_____ 11. Sarcasm   K. Anything fit to be eaten

_____ 12. Diversionary   L. Burning

_____ 13. Bland   M. Being alone

_____ 14. Psychological   N. Serving to distract the attention

_____ 15. Necrosis   O. Tasteless

_____ 16. Solitary   P. A taunting or cutting remark

_____ 17. Trauma   Q. The death or decay of tissue in a part of the body

_____ 18. Bankruptcy   R. A card game

_____ 19. Needlepoint   S. Embroidery of threads upon a canvas

_____ 20. Liberated   T. Of the mind; mental

MULTIPLE CHOICE UNIT TEST 1 *Izzy, Willy-Nilly* Page 5

IV. Composition

The book *Izzy, Willy-Nilly* shows us many different kinds of relationships among people. Describe Izzy's relationship with each of the people listed below, and tell what Izzy learned or gained from her relationship with each person during the time of her recovery. Write one paragraph for each person, and provide details or examples from the book to support your statements.

        Suzy
        Rosamunde
        Francie
        Adelia
        Mrs. Lingard

ANSWER SHEET MULTIPLE CHOICE UNIT TEST 1   *Izzy, Willy-Nilly*

I. Matching	II. Multiple Choice	III. Vocabulary
1. ___	1. ___	1. ___
2. ___	2. ___	2. ___
3. ___	3. ___	3. ___
4. ___	4. ___	4. ___
5. ___	5. ___	5. ___
6. ___	6. ___	6. ___
7. ___	7. ___	7. ___
8. ___	8. ___	8. ___
9. ___	9. ___	9. ___
10. ___	10. ___	10. ___
11. ___		11. ___
12. ___		12. ___
13. ___		13. ___
14. ___		14. ___
15. ___		15. ___
16. ___		16. ___
17. ___		17. ___
18. ___		18. ___
19. ___		19. ___
20. ___		20. ___

ANSWER KEY MULTIPLE CHOICE UNIT TEST 1 *Izzy, Willy-Nilly*

I. Matching	II. Multiple Choice	III. Vocabulary
1. E	1. A	1. H
2. L	2. C	2. G
3. O	3. A	3. J
4. M	4. D	4. I
5. Q	5. D	5. K
6. S	6. A	6. L
7. R	7. C	7. R
8. K	8. B	8. A
9. D	9. D	9. B
10. P	10. C	10. C
11. H		11. P
12. G		12. N
13. I		13. O
14. N		14. T
15. A		15. Q
16. F		16. M
17. T		17. E
18. B		18. F
19. C		19. S
20. J		20. D

MULTIPLE CHOICE UNIT TEST 2 - Izzy, Willy-Nilly

I. Matching Unit Words. Write the letter of the correct description next to each unit word.

____ 1. Jealous A. Izzy's sister

____ 2. Dora B. Mrs. Lingard removes these from Izzy's closet

____ 3. Cry C. Suzy thinks Rosamunde is _____.

____ 4. Perfection D. A friend who avoids Izzy

____ 5. Nice E. What Lingards don't do

____ 6. Shoes F. An adjective that describes Izzy

____ 7. Marco G. Izzy becomes part of this group

____ 8. Rosamunde H. Tony's girlfriend

____ 9. A batik cloth I. Francie often feels this way

____ 10. Deborah J. A place to purchased handmade crafts

____ 11. Joel and Jack K. Izzy often feels this way

____ 12. The school paper staff L. What Rosamunde hangs on the hospital wall

____ 13. Cheerleader M. Izzy's psychological liaison nurse

____ 14. Lauren N. A character from David Copperfield

____ 15. Depressed O. Mrs. Lingard see her crying at the hospital

____ 16. Latin Club P. After drinking heavily, he drove Izzy home

____ 17. Treasure Trove Q. Izzy envies Georgie's _____.

____ 18. Francie R. Izzy's twin brothers

____ 19. Not Cool S. Izzy was a _____.

____ 20. Mrs. Hughes-Pickne T. A school activity Izzy misses

MULTIPLE CHOICE UNIT TEST 2 – Izzy, Willy-Nilly Page 2

II. Multiple Choice.

1. Why did Izzy's parents not want her to go out with Marco?
    a. The twins did not like him.
    b. He was trouble.
    c. They did not know him.
    d. He had been suspended from the football team for the rest of the season.

2. Why does Izzy's best friend, Suzy, call Izzy from the pay phone at school?
    a. She needs to explain Izzy's homework assignments.
    b. She tells Izzy how much everyone misses her at school.
    c. Suzy wants to tell Izzy that Marco is sorry and worried.
    d. Suzy calls from school so all of Izzy's friends can say hello too.

3. When Izzy wakes up in the darkness of the night, what does she do?
    a. Eat
    b. Watch television
    c. Cry
    d. Call her parents.

4. Izzy figures out that Suzy is wearing whose letter sweater?
    a. Tony's
    b. Marco's
    c. Joel's
    d. Billy's

5. Why is Izzy's mother a little concerned about Rosamunde?
    a. She is concerned because Rosamunde is teaching Izzy too much too soon, and she's worried Izzy will get hurt.
    b. She is concerned because Rosamunde is "not as outgoing as Izzy's other friends."
    c. She is concerned because Rosamunde is "so different, in everything, her attitudes, her background, her values."
    d. She is concerned because she has not met Rosamunde's parents.

6. What does Izzy tell Rosamunde and make her promise not to tell anyone?
    a. Izzy tells Rosamunde that she is often depressed and cries herself to sleep.
    b. Izzy tells Rosamunde that Suzy and Lauren no longer visit or call her.
    c. Izzy tells Rosamunde the truth about what happened the night of the accident.
    d. Izzy tells Rosamunde that she plans on transferring to a new school.

MULTIPLE CHOICE UNIT TEST 2 *Izzy, Willy-Nilly* Page 3

II. Multiple Choice (Cont.)

7. What homework assignment does Izzy have trouble understanding?
    a. She has trouble understanding the world history project requirements.
    b. She has trouble with the geometry proofs.
    c. She has trouble understanding what all the biology definitions mean.
    d. She has trouble understanding English, specifically the play Romeo and Juliet.

8. According to Joel, what does Jack underestimate in Izzy?
    a. He underestimates her persistence.
    b. He underestimates her forgiveness.
    c. He underestimates her brains.
    d. He underestimates her ability to get along with others.

9. While at school, what makes Izzy cry?
    a. Her Latin teacher yells at her for being late.
    b. She sees the cheerleaders practicing their new routine.
    c. Someone quickly cuts past her, and she falls on her face.
    d. Lauren does not talk to her.

10. When Izzy sees Marco and Georgie Lowe together, what question does she ask Georgie?
    a. "Are you going to go out with him?"
    b. "Are you impressed because he is a senior?"
    c. "Don't you know you're better than him?"
    d. "Do you want to know the truth?"

MULTIPLE CHOICE UNIT TEST 2 – Izzy, Willy-Nilly Page 4

III. Vocabulary: Match the vocabulary words to their dictionary definitions.

_____ 1. Diminutive   A. Bragging

_____ 2. Reluctance   B. Incapable; unskilled

_____ 3. Certifiable   C. Bruises

_____ 4. Domestic   D. Set free; released

_____ 5. Wailing   E. Very Small

_____ 6. Smoldering   F. The state of being unable to pay debts

_____ 7. Repressing   G. Kept from changing

_____ 8. Solitaire   H. Insane

_____ 9. Disjointed   I. Disconnected

_____ 10. Contusions   J. A card game played by one person

_____ 11. Incompetence   K. Anything fit to be eaten

_____ 12. Diversionary   L. Burning

_____ 13. Edible   M. Being alone

_____ 14. Psychological   N. Serving to distract the attention

_____ 15. Necrosis   O. Holding back

_____ 16. Solitary   P. Long pitiful crying

_____ 17. Boasting   Q. The death or decay of tissue in a part of the body

_____ 18. Bankruptcy   R. Having to do with the home or housekeeping

_____ 19. Stabilized   S. Unwillingness

_____ 20. Liberated   T. Of the mind; mental

MULTIPLE CHOICE UNIT TEST 2 *Izzy, Willy-Nilly* Page 5

IV. Essay

    Booklist's review of *Izzy, Willy-Nilly* says, "Conveys a keen understanding of the physical practicalities involved in coping with a handicap."

    Use this statement as the thesis of your essay, and support it using specific examples from the book.

ANSWER SHEET MULTIPLE CHOICE UNIT TEST 2   *Izzy, Willy-Nilly*

I. Matching	II. Multiple Choice	III. Vocabulary
1. ___	1. ___	1. ___
2. ___	2. ___	2. ___
3. ___	3. ___	3. ___
4. ___	4. ___	4. ___
5. ___	5. ___	5. ___
6. ___	6. ___	6. ___
7. ___	7. ___	7. ___
8. ___	8. ___	8. ___
9. ___	9. ___	9. ___
10. ___	10. ___	10. ___
11. ___		11. ___
12. ___		12. ___
13. ___		13. ___
14. ___		14. ___
15. ___		15. ___
16. ___		16. ___
17. ___		17. ___
18. ___		18. ___
19. ___		19. ___
20. ___		20. ___

ANSWER SHEET MULTIPLE CHOICE UNIT TEST 2   *Izzy, Willy-Nilly*

I. Matching	II. Multiple Choice	III. Vocabulary
1. I	1. C	1. E
2. N	2. C	2. S
3. E	3. C	3. H
4. Q	4. B	4. R
5. F	5. C	5. P
6. B	6. C	6. L
7. P	7. D	7. O
8. O	8. C	8. J
9. L	9. C	9. I
10. H	10. A	10. C
11. R		11. B
12. G		12. N
13. S		13. K
14. D		14. T
15. K		15. Q
16. T		16. M
17. J		17. A
18. A		18. F
19. C		19. G
20. M		20. D

UNIT RESOURCE MATERIALS

BULLETIN BOARD IDEAS *Izzy, Willy-Nilly*

1. Save one corner of the board for the best of students' *Izzy, Willy-Nilly* writing assignments.

2. Take one of the word search puzzles from the extra activities packet and with a marker copy it over in a large size on the bulletin board. Write the clue words to find to one side. Invite students prior to and after class to find the words and circle them on the bulletin board.

3. Write several of the most significant quotations from the book onto the board on brightly colored paper.

4. Make a bulletin board listing the vocabulary words for this unit. As you complete sections of the novel and discuss the vocabulary for each section, write the definitions on the bulletin board. (If your board is one students face frequently, it will help them learn the words.)

5. Have students research famous disabled people. Display each person's photograph and a brief biography.

6. Display a list of Cynthia Voigt's other books. Include a brief description of each book.

7. Display each group's school accessibility checklist findings (see lessons 12 and 13).

8. Have students research some of the famous people referred to in the book. Display their photos and biographies. Suggestions include: Ingmar Bergman, Barbara Walters, Jacqueline Kennedy Onassis, Mother Teresa, Mary Lou Retton, Agatha Christie, Shirley Temple, Roy Rogers, Ronald Reagan, Michael Jackson, Prince Andrew, Princess Di, Judy Blume, Robert Redford, Stevie Wonder, and Norman Rockwell.

EXTRA ACTIVITIES *Izzy, Willy-Nilly*

One of the difficulties in teaching a novel is that all students don't read at the same speed. One student who likes to read may take the book home and finish it in a day or two. Sometimes a few students finish the in-class assignments early. The problem, then, is finding suitable extra activities for students.

One thing that seems to help is to keep a little library in the classroom. For this unit, you might obtain the following books: *Teens with Physical Disabilities: Real-Life Stories of Meeting the Challenges* by Glenn Alan Cheney; *Fiddler to the World: The Inspiring Life of Itzhak Perlman* by Carol Behrman; *How it Feels to Live with a Physical Disability* by Jill Krementz; *One-Handed in a Two-Handed World* by Tommye Mayer. Other stories or articles about disabilities and/or disability awareness, would also be of interest. Consider books, articles, or web sites related to alcohol abuse, precautions to take when one goes to a party, or peer pressure. It might also be a good time to make available hotline numbers and information about alcohol or drug abuse or general counseling.

Other things you may keep on hand are puzzles. We have made some relating directly to *Izzy, Willy-Nilly* for you. Feel free to duplicate them for your students to use. Teacher's Pet Publications also publishes a Puzzle Pack™ which is filled with puzzles, games, and worksheets related to *Izzy, Willy-Nilly*.

Some students may like to draw. You might devise a contest or allow some extra-credit grade for students who draw characters or scenes from *Izzy,Willy-Nilly*. Note, too, that if the students do not want to keep their drawings you may pick up some extra bulletin board materials this way. If you have a contest and you supply the prize (a CD or something like that perhaps), you could, possibly, make the drawing itself a non-returnable entry fee.

The pages which follow contain games, puzzles and worksheets. The keys, when appropriate, immediately follow the puzzle or worksheet. There are two main groups of activities: one group for the unit; that is, generally relating to *Izzy, Willy-Nilly* text, and another group of activities related strictly to Izzy, Willy-Nilly vocabulary.

Directions for these games, puzzles and worksheets are self-explanatory. The object here is to provide you with extra materials you may use in any way you choose.

MORE ACTIVITIES   *Izzy, Willy-Nilly*

1. Have students work together to make a time line chronology of the events in the story. Take a large piece of construction paper and on one wall (or however you can physically arrange it in your room) and make the events of the story along it. Students may want to add drawings or cut-out pictures to represent the events (as well as a written statement).

2. Have students design a book cover (front and back and inside flaps) for *Izzy, Willy-Nilly*.

3. Have students design a bulletin board (ready to be put up; not just sketched) for *Izzy, Willy-Nilly*.

4. Have students group the books together to show the larger structure of the novel. Have them explain why they chose the divisions they made.

5. Have students choose one chapter of the book (with sufficient dialogue) to rewrite as a play. In conjunction with this assignment, have students write a composition explaining the difficulties they encountered in changing from one written form to another.

6. Have students research famous disabled people. Display each person's photograph along with a brief biography.

7. Have students make a concentration vocabulary game. Place students in groups of two or three, and provide each group with 40 index cards. Tell the group to select 20 vocabulary words from their *Izzy, Willy Nilly* vocabulary lists. Have each group member write a vocabulary word on one card and the corresponding definition on a different card. Once all 40 cards are made, students can play vocabulary concentration: Students shuffle the cards, place them face down, and find the matches. The player with the most matches wins.

8. You could also have them make concentration cards that match unit words to clues.

9. Assign Dickens' *David Copperfield* or Shakespeare's *Romeo and Juliet* to interested readers.

10. Have students research some of the famous people referred to in the book. Suggestions include: Ingmar Bergman, Barbara Walters, Jacqueline Kennedy Onassis, Mother Teresa, Mary Lou Retton, Agatha Christie, Shirley Temple, Roy Rogers, Ronald Reagan, Michael Jackson, Prince Andrew, Princess Di, Judy Blume, Robert Redford, Stevie Wonder, and Norman Rockwell.

WORD SEARCH Izzy, Willy-Nilly

```
C J V Y J Q C H E E R L E A D E R G T T
R J R M S F A U A T T G T J C P S R R C
U C J C H R L M V I H Z O R S R D I I P
T M R F O Q M I D X R E B A T I K G V W
C Y A B E D H L T X L C R S F M S G I F
H L E R S T K I T T J G U A Z N J E A X
E D K T C G R A R G L B L T P M Y R L W
S S N W Y O B T E P Z E A Z Z I P S W T
N U S F X F Q E A P M Y F M F D S N E F
M Z M P T C M D S N S W N T M K L T B S
K Y B G R R M W U F S T V Z W G N P B H
G W W D E V J N R C T B E D R O O M E Z
Q N N H X M H S E V G D S I L S Q D R F
C C T W X F B X K B F S F T N N X B T J
X O T W P Y Q G K R Y R R F L M S S H S
M F D F H V H F Z B L O M L P F C D T F
N P X G M X K M T L S S K X A C V W H V
Q C L B P Z N X P L G A V R L U W M D L
H L B V H K L F C C D M V A G D R B R W
H I B F B I R R B S T U S D E R Q E U Y
M N M J N C V P O Y C N B E L A T I N C
V G C G J R D E E M I D W L D J N O K L
N E A X A Q K N E A E E S I G H T I O J
F R A N C I E S R S U O L A E J P O C R
D O R A K B V B T L O O K S W B P H X E
```

ADELIA	DORA	JOEL	MOTHER	THERAPIST
BATIK	DRUNK	LATIN	NICE	TONY
BEDROOM	EPSTEIN	LAUREN	PENS	TREASURE
BRAINS	FRANCIE	LEFT	PIZZA	TREE
CHEERLEADER	GRIGGERS	LEG	POOL	TRIVIAL
CLINGER	HAIRCUT	LINGARD	ROMEO	WEBBER
CRUTCHES	HUMILIATED	LITTLE	ROSAMUNDE	
CRY	JACK	LOOKS	SHOES	
DEBORAH	JEALOUS	MARCO	SUZY	

132

WORD SEARCH ANSWER KEY Izzy, Willy-Nilly

```
C        Y        C H E E R L E A D E R   G   T
R    R   S  A  T       J           R   R
U  C   H R  M  R  B A T I K        G   I
T  M   O L  I  L  R   A   P        G   V
C  A B E    T  E  U   T  Z I P S   E   I
H  E S C  O T  A  F   T         S  R   A
E D    U    R  P  T                    L
S U    R    E  S                       W
  Z    E       T                       E
  Y    H    B E D R O O M              B
       T         I                     B
     M O         N                     E
                                       R
                     R       L
  C                  O       A
  L       N          S     G R         D
  I       I          A   A E U       Y
  N   N   J       M  M D L A T I N   K
  G   G   A     E I  U E   A   N O   L
  E   A   A     R A  N I       T I   O
F R A N C I E S   E  D O       O     C
D O R A K     B T L  E O K S   P     E
```

ADELIA	DORA	JOEL	MOTHER	THERAPIST
BATIK	DRUNK	LATIN	NICE	TONY
BEDROOM	EPSTEIN	LAUREN	PENS	TREASURE
BRAINS	FRANCIE	LEFT	PIZZA	TREE
CHEERLEADER	GRIGGERS	LEG	POOL	TRIVIAL
CLINGER	HAIRCUT	LINGARD	ROMEO	WEBBER
CRUTCHES	HUMILIATED	LITTLE	ROSAMUNDE	
CRY	JACK	LOOKS	SHOES	
DEBORAH	JEALOUS	MARCO	SUZY	

CROSSWORD Izzy, Willy-Nilly

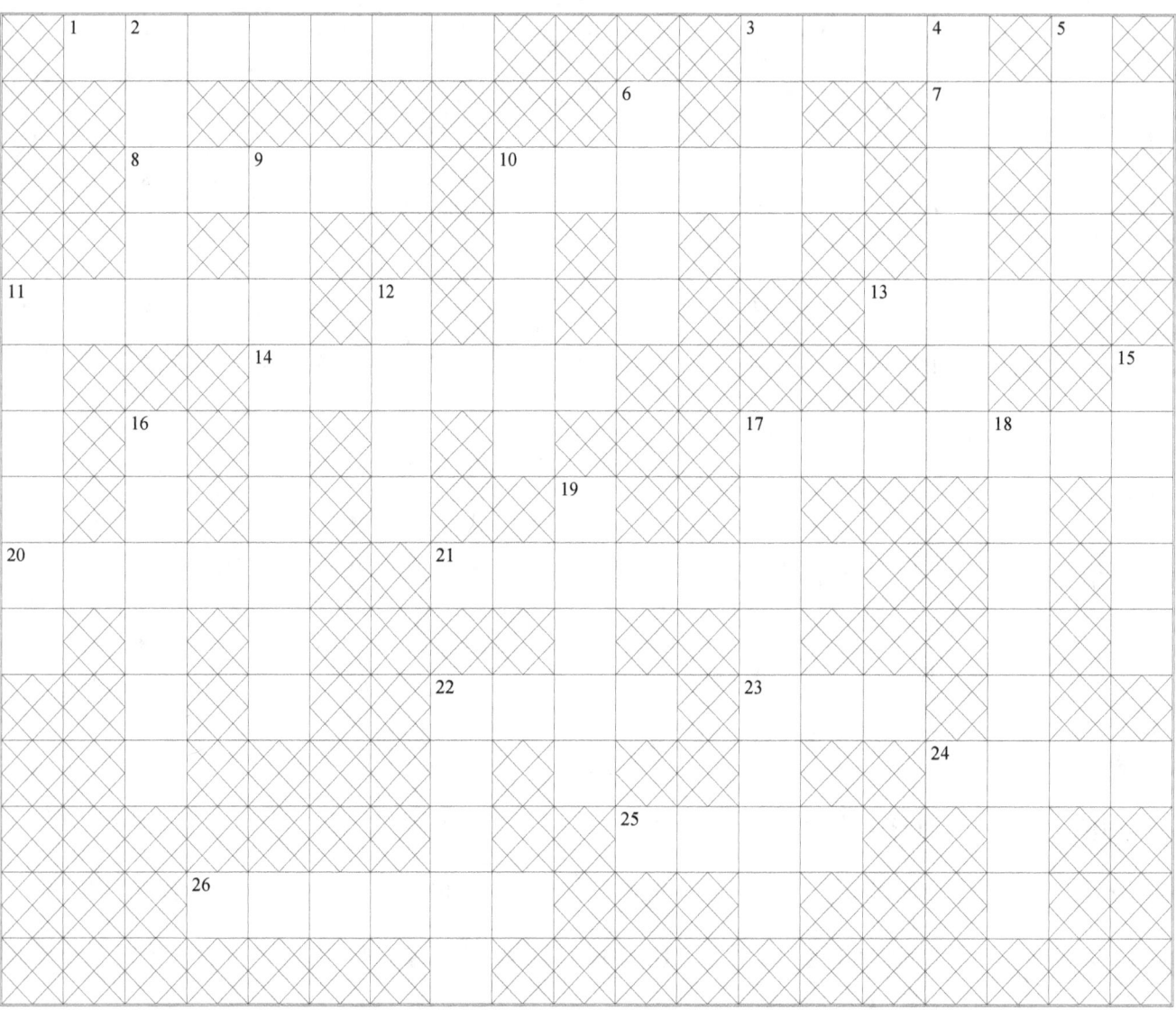

Across
1. Game Izzy, her siblings, & Rosamunde play: ___ Pursuit
3. Object the car ran into
7. Mr. Lingard wants to put one in the back yard
8. He was responsible for the car accident.
10. According to Joel, Jack underestimates Izzy's.
11. Mrs. Lingard thinks Rosamunde must be uncomfortable because of the way she ___.
13. Half of Izzy's right one was amputated.
14. Izzy's physical therapy nurse
17. Mrs. Lingard describes Rosamunde as a ___.
20. Club Izzy misses
21. What Izzy wants to give Rosamunde for Christmas
22. She calls Izzy to see if Izzy is going to tell that Marco had been drinking.
23. Lingards don't do this.
24. The row of ___ shoes in the closet makes Rosamunde laugh.
25. Twin brother who does visit Izzy
26. Rosamunde's last name

Down
2. The assignment for ___ & Juliet gives Izzy trouble.
3. He invites Izzy to join the newspaper staff
4. Doctor who is Izzy's pediatrician
5. Dr. Epstein compares Izzy to this Dickens character
6. Twin brother who does not visit Izzy in the hospital
9. Smart girl who becomes Izzy's friend
10. Rosamunde hangs an animal ___ on the hospital wall.
11. Izzy envisions ___ Izzy in her mind.
12. Izzy wants to borrow Francie's
15. Word describing Marco when he drove Izzy home
16. A good ___ would stay.
17. Little Izzy did a back flip when Tony forgot to bring Izzy these.
18. Marco's last name
19. Food Izzy wants to eat when she gets home
22. Mrs. Lingard removed all of Izzy's right ones from the closet.

CROSSWORD ANSWER KEY Izzy, Willy-Nilly

	1	2						3		4		5	
	T	R	I	V	I	A	L		T	R	E	E		D
		O					6		O		7		
		O					J		O		P	O	O	L
	8		9			10							
	M	A	R	C	O	B	R	A	I	N	S		R
		E		O		A		C		Y		T		A
11	L	O	O	K	S	12 P	T	K		13 L	E	G	
I			14 A	D	E	L	I	A			I		15 D
T	16 M	M	N		K			17 C	L	I	18 N	G	E	R
T	O	U	S		19 P			R			R		U
20 L	A	T	I	N	21 H	A	I	R	C	U	T		I		N
E	H	D				Z		T				G		K
	E	E		22 S	U	Z	Y		23 C	R	Y	G	
	R			H		A			H		24 L	E	F	T
				O				25 J	O	E	L	R	
	26 W	E	B	B	E	R			S			S	
				S									

Across
1. Game Izzy, her siblings, & Rosamunde play: ___ Pursuit
3. Object the car ran into
7. Mr. Lingard wants to put one in the back yard
8. He was responsible for the car accident.
10. According to Joel, Jack underestimates Izzy's.
11. Mrs. Lingard thinks Rosamunde must be uncomfortable because of the way she ___.
13. Half of Izzy's right one was amputated.
14. Izzy's physical therapy nurse
17. Mrs. Lingard describes Rosamunde as a ___.
20. Club Izzy misses
21. What Izzy wants to give Rosamunde for Christmas
22. She calls Izzy to see if Izzy is going to tell that Marco had been drinking.
23. Lingards don't do this.
24. The row of ___ shoes in the closet makes Rosamunde laugh.
25. Twin brother who does visit Izzy
26. Rosamunde's last name

Down
2. The assignment for ___ & Juliet gives Izzy trouble.
3. He invites Izzy to join the newspaper staff
4. Doctor who is Izzy's pediatrician
5. Dr. Epstein compares Izzy to this Dickens character
6. Twin brother who does not visit Izzy in the hospital
9. Smart girl who becomes Izzy's friend
10. Rosamunde hangs an animal ___ on the hospital wall.
11. Izzy envisions ___ Izzy in her mind.
12. Izzy wants to borrow Francie's
15. Word describing Marco when he drove Izzy home
16. A good ___ would stay.
17. Little Izzy did a back flip when Tony forgot to bring Izzy these.
18. Marco's last name
19. Food Izzy wants to eat when she gets home
22. Mrs. Lingard removed all of Izzy's right ones from the closet.

MATCHING 1 Izzy, Willy-Nilly

___ 1. SHOES   A. Friend who avoids Izzy

___ 2. SUZY   B. She calls Izzy to see if Izzy is going to tell that Marco had been drinking.

___ 3. HUMILIATED   C. Little Izzy did a back flip when Tony forgot to bring Izzy these.

___ 4. LATIN   D. Mrs. Lingard describes Rosamunde as a ___.

___ 5. THERAPIST   E. Doctor who is Izzy's pediatrician

___ 6. DEBORAH   F. Izzy's little sister

___ 7. CRY   G. Club Izzy misses

___ 8. FRANCIE   H. Francie had been ___ of Izzy before the accident.

___ 9. DRUNK   I. Twin brother who does not visit Izzy in the hospital

___10. LAUREN   J. Lingards don't do this.

___11. LINGARD   K. Mrs. Hughes-Pincke, for example

___12. CHEERLEADER   L. What Izzy wants to give Rosamunde for Christmas

___13. GRIGGERS   M. Tony's girlfriend

___14. TREASURE   N. Dr. Epstein compares Izzy to this Dickens character

___15. MOTHER   O. How Izzy feels when she falls at school

___16. JACK   P. Word describing Marco when he drove Izzy home

___17. EPSTEIN   Q. Former extra-curricular activity Izzy participated in

___18. CLINGER   R. Mrs. Lingard removed all of Izzy's right ones from the closet.

___19. JEALOUS   S. Izzy moves into her parents' on the first floor.

___20. HAIRCUT   T. Izzy's last name

___21. CRUTCHES   U. Izzy wants to borrow Francie's

___22. PENS   V. A good ___ would stay.

___23. ADELIA   W. Place to buy handmade crafts: ___ Trove

___24. DORA   X. Marco's last name

___25. BEDROOM   Y. Izzy's physical therapy nurse

MATCHING 1 ANSWER KEY Izzy, Willy-Nilly

R - 1.	SHOES	A. Friend who avoids Izzy
B - 2.	SUZY	B. She calls Izzy to see if Izzy is going to tell that Marco had been drinking.
O - 3.	HUMILIATED	C. Little Izzy did a back flip when Tony forgot to bring Izzy these.
G - 4.	LATIN	D. Mrs. Lingard describes Rosamunde as a ___.
K - 5.	THERAPIST	E. Doctor who is Izzy's pediatrician
M - 6.	DEBORAH	F. Izzy's little sister
J - 7.	CRY	G. Club Izzy misses
F - 8.	FRANCIE	H. Francie had been ___ of Izzy before the accident.
P - 9.	DRUNK	I. Twin brother who does not visit Izzy in the hospital
A -10.	LAUREN	J. Lingards don't do this.
T -11.	LINGARD	K. Mrs. Hughes-Pincke, for example
Q -12.	CHEERLEADER	L. What Izzy wants to give Rosamunde for Christmas
X -13.	GRIGGERS	M. Tony's girlfriend
W 14.	TREASURE	N. Dr. Epstein compares Izzy to this Dickens character
V -15.	MOTHER	O. How Izzy feels when she falls at school
I - 16.	JACK	P. Word describing Marco when he drove Izzy home
E -17.	EPSTEIN	Q. Former extra-curricular activity Izzy participated in
D -18.	CLINGER	R. Mrs. Lingard removed all of Izzy's right ones from the closet.
H -19.	JEALOUS	S. Izzy moves into her parents' on the first floor.
L -20.	HAIRCUT	T. Izzy's last name
C -21.	CRUTCHES	U. Izzy wants to borrow Francie's
U -22.	PENS	V. A good ___ would stay.
Y -23.	ADELIA	W. Place to buy handmade crafts: ___ Trove
N -24.	DORA	X. Marco's last name
S -25.	BEDROOM	Y. Izzy's physical therapy nurse

MATCHING 2 Izzy, Willy-Nilly

___ 1. PIZZA   A. Object the car ran into

___ 2. POOL   B. Izzy wants to borrow Francie's

___ 3. ADELIA   C. Marco's last name

___ 4. DRUNK   D. Half of Izzy's right one was amputated.

___ 5. LINGARD   E. Izzy's last name

___ 6. ROSAMUNDE   F. Izzy's little sister

___ 7. THERAPIST   G. Former extra-curricular activity Izzy participated in

___ 8. TREE   H. Rosamunde hangs an animal ___ on the hospital wall.

___ 9. LAUREN   I. Mrs. Lingard thinks Rosamunde must be uncomfortable because of the way she ___.

___ 10. EPSTEIN   J. Place to buy handmade crafts: ___ Trove

___ 11. BRAINS   K. Mrs. Hughes-Pincke, for example

___ 12. HUMILIATED   L. Lingards don't do this.

___ 13. TONY   M. Doctor who is Izzy's pediatrician

___ 14. LEG   N. Food Izzy wants to eat when she gets home

___ 15. CLINGER   O. Twin brother who does not visit Izzy in the hospital

___ 16. TREASURE   P. Dr. Epstein compares Izzy to this Dickens character

___ 17. FRANCIE   Q. Mrs. Lingard describes Rosamunde as a ___.

___ 18. DORA   R. Friend who avoids Izzy

___ 19. CHEERLEADER   S. How Izzy feels when she falls at school

___ 20. GRIGGERS   T. Word describing Marco when he drove Izzy home

___ 21. PENS   U. Mr. Lingard wants to put one in the back yard

___ 22. BATIK   V. According to Joel, Jack underestimates Izzy's.

___ 23. LOOKS   W. Izzy's physical therapy nurse

___ 24. CRY   X. He invites Izzy to join the newspaper staff

___ 25. JACK   Y. Smart girl who becomes Izzy's friend

MATCHING 2 ANSWER KEY Izzy, Willy-Nilly

N - 1.	PIZZA	A. Object the car ran into
U - 2.	POOL	B. Izzy wants to borrow Francie's
W 3.	ADELIA	C. Marco's last name
T - 4.	DRUNK	D. Half of Izzy's right one was amputated.
E - 5.	LINGARD	E. Izzy's last name
Y - 6.	ROSAMUNDE	F. Izzy's little sister
K - 7.	THERAPIST	G. Former extra-curricular activity Izzy participated in
A - 8.	TREE	H. Rosamunde hangs an animal ___ on the hospital wall.
R - 9.	LAUREN	I. Mrs. Lingard thinks Rosamunde must be uncomfortable because of the way she ___.
M -10.	EPSTEIN	J. Place to buy handmade crafts: ___ Trove
V -11.	BRAINS	K. Mrs. Hughes-Pincke, for example
S -12.	HUMILIATED	L. Lingards don't do this.
X -13.	TONY	M. Doctor who is Izzy's pediatrician
D -14.	LEG	N. Food Izzy wants to eat when she gets home
Q -15.	CLINGER	O. Twin brother who does not visit Izzy in the hospital
J - 16.	TREASURE	P. Dr. Epstein compares Izzy to this Dickens character
F -17.	FRANCIE	Q. Mrs. Lingard describes Rosamunde as a ___.
P -18.	DORA	R. Friend who avoids Izzy
G -19.	CHEERLEADER	S. How Izzy feels when she falls at school
C -20.	GRIGGERS	T. Word describing Marco when he drove Izzy home
B -21.	PENS	U. Mr. Lingard wants to put one in the back yard
H -22.	BATIK	V. According to Joel, Jack underestimates Izzy's.
I - 23.	LOOKS	W. Izzy's physical therapy nurse
L -24.	CRY	X. He invites Izzy to join the newspaper staff
O -25.	JACK	Y. Smart girl who becomes Izzy's friend

JUGGLE LETTERS Izzy, Willy-Nilly

1. FNACRIE   = 1. _____
                         Izzy's little sister

2. TILLTE   = 2. _____
                         Izzy envisions ___ Izzy in her mind.

3. IRIATLV   = 3. _____
                         Game Izzy, her siblings, & Rosamunde play: ___ Pursuit

4. REET   = 4. _____
                         Object the car ran into

5. AUTRHCI   = 5. _____
                         What Izzy wants to give Rosamunde for Christmas

6. EOJL   = 6. _____
                         Twin brother who does visit Izzy

7. ADERBHO   = 7. _____
                         Tony's girlfriend

8. KAJC   = 8. _____
                         Twin brother who does not visit Izzy in the hospital

9. ERUALN   = 9. _____
                         Friend who avoids Izzy

10. OOPL   =10. _____
                         Mr. Lingard wants to put one in the back yard

11. LHAEEREECRD   =11. _____
                         Former extra-curricular activity Izzy participated in

12. OHRTME   =12. _____
                         A good ___ would stay.

13. OSSEH   =13. _____
                         Mrs. Lingard removed all of Izzy's right ones from the closet.

14. SAIBRN   =14. _____
                         According to Joel, Jack underestimates Izzy's.

15. FETL   =15. _____
                         The row of ___ shoes in the closet makes Rosamunde laugh.

16. NODMSUEAR =16. _____
Smart girl who becomes Izzy's friend

17. SPNE =17. _____
Izzy wants to borrow Francie's

18. YUZS =18. _____
She calls Izzy to see if Izzy is going to tell that Marco had been drinking.

19. DREMBOO =19. _____
Izzy moves into her parents' on the first floor.

20. OOLSK =20. _____
Mrs. Lingard thinks Rosamunde must be uncomfortable because of the way she ___.

21. RSREGIGG =21. _____
Marco's last name

22. EBWEBR =22. _____
Rosamunde's last name

23. ZPIAZ =23. _____
Food Izzy wants to eat when she gets home

24. YOTN =24. _____
He invites Izzy to join the newspaper staff

25. INESTPE =25. _____
Doctor who is Izzy's pediatrician

26. ECNI =26. _____
Word describing Izzy

27. KIATB =27. _____
Rosamunde hangs an animal ___ on the hospital wall.

28. PESTRTIHA =28. _____
Mrs. Hughes-Pincke, for example

29. EDLMHTAIIU =29. _____
How Izzy feels when she falls at school

30. ARGLNID =30. _____
Izzy's last name

31. INLGCER =31. _____

Mrs. Lingard describes Rosamunde as a ___.

32. ASJEULO =32. _____

Francie had been ___ of Izzy before the accident.

33. ORAMC =33. _____

He was responsible for the car accident.

34. ERAESUTR =34. _____

Place to buy handmade crafts: ___ Trove

35. MOROE =35. _____

The assignment for ___ & Juliet gives Izzy trouble.

36. YRC =36. _____

Lingards don't do this.

37. CUTSHREC =37. _____

Little Izzy did a back flip when Tony forgot to bring Izzy these.

38. GEL =38. _____

Half of Izzy's right one was amputated.

JUGGLE LETTER ANSWER KEY Izzy, Willy-Nilly

1. FNACRIE = 1. FRANCIE
   Izzy's little sister

2. TILLTE = 2. LITTLE
   Izzy envisions ___ Izzy in her mind.

3. IRIATLV = 3. TRIVIAL
   Game Izzy, her siblings, & Rosamunde play: ___ Pursuit

4. REET = 4. TREE
   Object the car ran into

5. AUTRHCI = 5. HAIRCUT
   What Izzy wants to give Rosamunde for Christmas

6. EOJL = 6. JOEL
   Twin brother who does visit Izzy

7. ADERBHO = 7. DEBORAH
   Tony's girlfriend

8. KAJC = 8. JACK
   Twin brother who does not visit Izzy in the hospital

9. ERUALN = 9. LAUREN
   Friend who avoids Izzy

10. OOPL = 10. POOL
    Mr. Lingard wants to put one in the back yard

11. LHAEEREECRD = 11. CHEERLEADER
    Former extra-curricular activity Izzy participated in

12. OHRTME = 12. MOTHER
    A good ___ would stay.

13. OSSEH = 13. SHOES
    Mrs. Lingard removed all of Izzy's right ones from the closet.

14. SAIBRN = 14. BRAINS
    According to Joel, Jack underestimates Izzy's.

15. FETL = 15. LEFT
    The row of ___ shoes in the closet makes Rosamunde laugh.

16. NODMSUEAR =16. ROSAMUNDE

Smart girl who becomes Izzy's friend

17. SPNE =17. PENS

Izzy wants to borrow Francie's

18. YUZS =18. SUZY

She calls Izzy to see if Izzy is going to tell that Marco had been drinking.

19. DREMBOO =19. BEDROOM

Izzy moves into her parents' ___ on the first floor.

20. OOLSK =20. LOOKS

Mrs. Lingard thinks Rosamunde must be uncomfortable because of the way she ___.

21. RSREGIGG =21. GRIGGERS

Marco's last name

22. EBWEBR =22. WEBBER

Rosamunde's last name

23. ZPIAZ =23. PIZZA

Food Izzy wants to eat when she gets home

24. YOTN =24. TONY

He invites Izzy to join the newspaper staff

25. INESTPE =25. EPSTEIN

Doctor who is Izzy's pediatrician

26. ECNI =26. NICE

Word describing Izzy

27. KIATB =27. BATIK

Rosamunde hangs an animal ___ on the hospital wall.

28. PESTRTIHA =28. THERAPIST

Mrs. Hughes-Pincke, for example

29. EDLMHTAIIU =29. HUMILIATED

How Izzy feels when she falls at school

30. ARGLNID =30. LINGARD

Izzy's last name

31. INLGCER =31. CLINGER

Mrs. Lingard describes Rosamunde as a ___.

32. ASJEULO =32. JEALOUS

Francie had been ___ of Izzy before the accident.

33. ORAMC =33. MARCO

He was responsible for the car accident.

34. ERAESUTR =34. TREASURE

Place to buy handmade crafts: ___ Trove

35. MOROE =35. ROMEO

The assignment for ___ & Juliet gives Izzy trouble.

36. YRC =36. CRY

Lingards don't do this.

37. CUTSHREC =37. CRUTCHES

Little Izzy did a back flip when Tony forgot to bring Izzy these.

38. GEL =38. LEG

Half of Izzy's right one was amputated.

Izzy, Willy-Nilly Unit Word List

No.	Word	Clue/Definition
1.	ADELIA	Izzy's physical therapy nurse
2.	BATIK	Rosamunde hangs an animal ___ on the hospital wall.
3.	BEDROOM	Izzy moves into her parents' on the first floor.
4.	BRAINS	According to Joel, Jack underestimates Izzy's.
5.	CHEERLEADER	Former extra-curricular activity Izzy participated in
6.	CLINGER	Mrs. Lingard describes Rosamunde as a ___.
7.	CRUTCHES	Little Izzy did a back flip when Tony forgot to bring Izzy these.
8.	CRY	Lingards don't do this.
9.	DEBORAH	Tony's girlfriend
10.	DORA	Dr. Epstein compares Izzy to this Dickens character
11.	DRUNK	Word describing Marco when he drove Izzy home
12.	EPSTEIN	Doctor who is Izzy's pediatrician
13.	FRANCIE	Izzy's little sister
14.	GRIGGERS	Marco's last name
15.	HAIRCUT	What Izzy wants to give Rosamunde for Christmas
16.	HUMILIATED	How Izzy feels when she falls at school
17.	JACK	Twin brother who does not visit Izzy in the hospital
18.	JEALOUS	Francie had been ___ of Izzy before the accident.
19.	JOEL	Twin brother who does visit Izzy
20.	LATIN	Club Izzy misses
21.	LAUREN	Friend who avoids Izzy
22.	LEFT	The row of ___ shoes in the closet makes Rosamunde laugh.
23.	LEG	Half of Izzy's right one was amputated.
24.	LINGARD	Izzy's last name
25.	LITTLE	Izzy envisions ___ Izzy in her mind.
26.	LOOKS	Mrs. Lingard thinks Rosamunde must be uncomfortable because of the way she ___.
27.	MARCO	He was responsible for the car accident.
28.	MOTHER	A good ___ would stay.
29.	NICE	Word describing Izzy
30.	PENS	Izzy wants to borrow Francie's
31.	PIZZA	Food Izzy wants to eat when she gets home
32.	POOL	Mr. Lingard wants to put one in the back yard
33.	ROMEO	The assignment for ___ & Juliet gives Izzy trouble.
34.	ROSAMUNDE	Smart girl who becomes Izzy's friend
35.	SHOES	Mrs. Lingard removed all of Izzy's right ones from the closet.
36.	SUZY	She calls Izzy to see if Izzy is going to tell that Marco had been drinking.
37.	THERAPIST	Mrs. Hughes-Pincke, for example
38.	TONY	He invites Izzy to join the newspaper staff
39.	TREASURE	Place to buy handmade crafts: ___ Trove
40.	TREE	Object the car ran into
41.	TRIVIAL	Game Izzy, her siblings, & Rosamunde play: ___ Pursuit
42.	WEBBER	Rosamunde's last name

U.S. Department of Justice
Civil Rights Division
Disability Rights Section

A GUIDE TO DISABILITY RIGHTS LAWS

September 2005

TABLE OF CONTENTS

Americans with Disabilities Act..	1
Telecommunications Act...	8
Fair Housing Act..	9
Air Carrier Access Act...	11
Voting Accessibility for the Elderly and Handicapped Act..	12
National Voter Registration Act...	13
Civil Rights of Institutionalized Persons Act..	14
Individuals with Disabilities Education Act..	15
Rehabilitation Act..	16
Architectural Barriers Act..	19
General Sources of Disability Rights Information..	19
Statute Citations..	20

For persons with disabilities, this document is available in large print, Braille, audio tape, and computer disk.

Reproduction of this document is encouraged.

This guide provides an overview of Federal civil rights laws that ensure equal opportunity for people with disabilities. To find outmore about how these laws may apply to you, contact the agencies and organizations listed below.

Americans with Disabilities Act (ADA)

The ADA prohibits discrimination on the basis of disability in employment, State and local government, public accommodations, commercial facilities, transportation, and telecommunications. It also applies to the United States Congress.

To be protected by the ADA, one must have a disability or have a relationship or association with an individual with a disability. An individual with a disability is defined by the ADA as a person who has a physical or mental impairment that substantially limits one or more major life activities, a person who has a history or record of such an impairment, or a person who is perceived by others as having such an impairment. The ADA does not specifically name all of the impairments that are covered.

ADA Title I: Employment

Title I requires employers with 15 or more employees to provide qualified individuals with disabilities an equal opportunity to benefit from the full range of employment-related opportunities available to others. For example, it prohibits discrimination in recruitment, hiring, promotions, training, pay, social activities, and other privileges of employment. It restricts questions that can be asked about an applicant's disability before a job offer is made, and it requires that employers make reasonable accommodation to the known physical or mental limitations of otherwise qualified individuals with disabilities, unless it results in undue hardship. Religious entities with 15 or more employees are covered under title I.

Title I complaints must be filed with the U. S. Equal Employment Opportunity Commission (EEOC) within 180 days of the date of discrimination, or 300 days if the charge is filed with a designated State or local fair employment practice agency. Individuals may file a lawsuit in Federal court only after they receive a "right-to-sue" letter from the EEOC.

Charges of employment discrimination on the basis of disability may be filed at any U.S. Equal Employment Opportunity Commission field office. Field offices are located in 50 cities throughout the U.S. and are listed in most telephone directories under "U.S. Government." For the appropriate EEOC field office in your geographic area, contact:
(800) 669-4000 (voice)
(800) 669-6820 (TTY)

www.eeoc.gov

Publications and information on EEOC-enforced laws may be obtained by calling:

(800) 669-3362 (voice)
(800) 800-3302 (TTY)

For information on how to accommodate a specific individual with a disability, contact the Job Accommodation Network at:

(800) 526-7234 (voice/TTY)

www.jan.wvu.edu

ADA Title II: State and Local Government Activities

Title II covers all activities of State and local governments regardless of the government entity's size or receipt of Federal funding. Title II requires that State and local governments give people with disabilities an equal opportunity to benefit from all of their programs, services, and activities (e.g. public education, employment, transportation, recreation, health care, social services, courts, voting, and town meetings).

State and local governments are required to follow specific architectural standards in the new construction and alteration of their buildings. They also must relocate programs or otherwise provide access in inaccessible older buildings, and communicate effectively with people who have hearing, vision, or speech disabilities. Public entities are not required to take actions that would result in undue financial and administrative burdens. They are required to make reasonable modifications to policies, practices, and procedures where necessary to avoid discrimination, unless they can demonstrate that doing so would fundamentally alter the nature of the service, program, or activity being provided.

Complaints of title II violations may be filed with the Department of Justice within 180 days of the date of discrimination. In certain situations, cases may be referred to a mediation program sponsored by the Department. The Department may bring a lawsuit where it has investigated a matter and has been unable to resolve violations. For more information, contact:

U.S. Department of Justice
Civil Rights Division
950 Pennsylvania Avenue, N.W.
Disability Rights Section - NYAV
Washington, D.C. 20530

www.ada.gov

(800) 514-0301 (voice)
(800) 514-0383 (TTY)

Title II may also be enforced through private lawsuits in Federal court. It is not necessary to file a complaint with the Department of Justice (DOJ) or any other Federal agency, or to receive a "right-to-sue" letter, before going to court.

ADA Title II: Public Transportation

The transportation provisions of title II cover public transportation services, such as city buses and public rail transit (e.g. subways, commuter rails, Amtrak). Public transportation authorities may not discriminate against people with disabilities in the provision of their services. They must comply with requirements for accessibility in newly purchased vehicles, make good faith efforts to purchase or lease accessible used buses, remanufacture buses in an accessible manner, and, unless it would result in an undue burden, provide paratransit where they operate fixed-route bus or rail systems. Paratransit is a service where individuals who are unable to use the regular transit system independently (because of a physical or mental impairment) are picked up and dropped off at their destinations. Questions and complaints about public transportation should be directed to:

> Office of Civil Rights
> Federal Transit Administration
> U.S. Department of Transportation
> 400 Seventh Street, S.W., Room 9102
> Washington, D.C. 20590
>
> www.fta.dot.gov/ada
>
> (888) 446-4511 (voice/relay)

ADA Title III: Public Accommodations

Title III covers businesses and nonprofit service providers that are public accommodations, privately operated entities offering certain types of courses and examinations, privately operated transportation, and commercial facilities. Public accommodations are private entities who own, lease, lease to, or operate facilities such as restaurants, retail stores, hotels, movie theaters, private schools, convention centers, doctors' offices, homeless shelters, transportation depots, zoos, funeral homes, day care centers, and recreation facilities including sports stadiums and fitness clubs. Transportation services provided by private entities are also covered by title III.

Public accommodations must comply with basic nondiscrimination requirements that prohibit exclusion, segregation, and unequal treatment. They also must comply with specific requirements related to architectural standards for new and altered buildings; reasonable modifications to policies, practices, and procedures; effective communication with people with hearing, vision, or speech disabilities; and other access requirements. Additionally, public accommodations must remove barriers in existing buildings where it is easy to do so without much difficulty or expense, given the public accommodation's resources.

Courses and examinations related to professional, educational, or trade-related applications, licensing, certifications, or credentialing must be provided in a place and manner accessible to people with disabilities, or alternative accessible arrangements must be offered.

Commercial facilities, such as factories and warehouses, must comply with the ADA's architectural standards for new construction and alterations.

Complaints of title III violations may be filed with the Department of Justice. In certain situations, cases may be referred to a mediation program sponsored by the Department. The Department is authorized to bring a lawsuit where there is a pattern or practice of discrimination in violation of title III, or where an act of discrimination raises an issue of general public importance. Title III may also be enforced through private lawsuits. It is not necessary to file a complaint with the Department of Justice (or any Federal agency), or to receive a "right-to-sue" letter, before going to court. For more information, contact:

> U.S. Department of Justice
> Civil Rights Division
> 950 Pennsylvania Avenue, N.W.
> Disability Rights Section - NYAV
> Washington, D.C. 20530
>
> www.ada.gov
>
> (800) 514-0301 (voice)
> (800) 514-0383 (TTY)

ADA Title IV: Telecommunications Relay Services

Title IV addresses telephone and television access for people with hearing and speech disabilities. It requires common carriers(telephone companies) to establish interstate and intrastate telecommunications relay services (TRS) 24 hours a day, 7 days a week. TRS enables callers with hearing and speech disabilities who use telecommunications devices for the deaf (TDDs), which are also known as teletypewriters (TTYs), and callers who use voice telephones to communicate with each other through a third party communications assistant. The Federal Communications Commission(FCC) has set minimum standards for TRS services. Title IV also requires closed captioning of Federally funded public service announcements. For more information about TRS, contact the FCC at:

> Federal Communications Commission
> 445 12th Street, S.W.
> Washington, D.C. 20554
>
> www.fcc.gov/cgb/dro
>
> (888) 225-5322 (Voice)
> (888) 835-5322 (TTY)

Telecommunications Act

Section 255 and Section 251(a)(2) of the Communications Act of 1934, as amended by the Telecommunications Act of 1996, require manufacturers of telecommunications equipment and providers of telecommunications services to ensure that such equipment and services are accessible to and usable by persons with disabilities, if readily achievable. These amendments ensure that people with disabilities will have access to a broad range of products and services such as telephones, cell phones, pagers, call-waiting, and operator services, that were often inaccessible to many users with disabilities. For more information, contact:

> Federal Communications Commission
> 445 12th Street, S.W.
> Washington, D.C. 20554
>
> www.fcc.gov/cgb/dro
>
> (888) 225-5322 (Voice)
> (888) 835-5322 (TTY)

Fair Housing Act

The Fair Housing Act, as amended in 1988, prohibits housing discrimination on the basis of race, color, religion, sex, disability, familial status, and national origin. Its coverage includes private housing, housing that receives Federal financial assistance, and State and local government housing. It is unlawful to discriminate in any aspect of selling or renting housing or to deny a dwelling to a buyer or renter because of the disability of that individual, an individual associated with the buyer or renter, or an individual who intends to live in the residence. Other covered activities include, for example, financing, zoning practices, new construction design, and advertising.

The Fair Housing Act requires owners of housing facilities to make reasonable exceptions in their policies and operations to afford people with disabilities equal housing opportunities. For example, a landlord with a "no pets" policy may be required to grant an exception to this rule and allow an individual who is blind to keep a guide dog in the residence. The Fair Housing Act also requires landlords to allow tenants with disabilities to make reasonable access-related modifications to their private living space, as well as to common use spaces. (The landlord is not required to pay for the changes.) The Act further requires that new multifamily housing with four or more units be designed and built to allow access for persons with disabilities. This includes accessible common use areas, doors that are wide enough for wheelchairs, kitchens and bathrooms that allow a person using a wheelchair to maneuver, and other adaptable features within the units.

Complaints of Fair Housing Act violations may be filed with the U.S. Department of Housing and Urban Development. For more information or to file a complaint, contact:

Office of Program Compliance and Disability Rights
Office of Fair Housing and Equal Opportunity
U.S. Department of Housing and Urban Development
451 7th Street, S.W., Room 5242
Washington, D.C. 20410

www.hud.gov/offices/fheo

(800) 669-9777 (voice)
(800) 927-9275 (TTY)

For questions about the accessibility provisions of the Fair Housing Act, you may contact Fair Housing Accessibility FIRST at:

www.fairhousingfirst.org

(888) 341-7781 (voice/TTY)

For publications, you may call the Housing and Urban Development Customer Service Center at:

(800) 767-7468 (voice/relay)

Additionally, the Department of Justice can file cases involving a pattern or practice of discrimination. The Fair Housing Act may also be enforced through private lawsuits.

Air Carrier Access Act

The Air Carrier Access Act prohibits discrimination in air transportation by domestic and foreign air carriers against qualified individuals with physical or mental impairments. It applies only to air carriers that provide regularly scheduled services for hire to the public. Requirements address a wide range of issues including boarding assistance and certain accessibility features in newly built aircraft and new or altered airport facilities. People may enforce rights under the Air Carrier Access Act by filing a complaint with the U.S. Department of Transportation, or by bringing a lawsuit in Federal court. For more information or to file a complaint, contact:

Aviation Consumer Protection Division
U.S. Department of Transportation
400 Seventh Street, S.W.
Room 4107, C-75
Washington, D.C. 20590

airconsumer.ost.dot.gov

(202) 366-2220 (voice)
(202) 366-0511 (TTY)

(800) 778-4838 (voice)
(800) 455-9880 (TTY)

Voting Accessibility for the Elderly and Handicapped Act

The Voting Accessibility for the Elderly and Handicapped Act of 1984 generally requires polling places across the United States to be physically accessible to people with disabilities for federal elections. Where no accessible location is available to serve as a polling place, a political subdivision must provide an alternate means of casting a ballot on the day of the election. This law also requires states to make available registration and voting aids for disabled and elderly voters, including information by telecommunications devices for the deaf (TDDs) which are also known as teletypewriters (TTYs). For more information, contact:

U.S. Department of Justice
Civil Rights Division
950 Pennsylvania Avenue, N.W.
Voting Section - 1800G
Washington, D.C. 20530

(800) 253-3931 (voice/TTY)

National Voter Registration Act

The National Voter Registration Act of 1993, also known as the "Motor Voter Act," makes it easier for all Americans to exercise their fundamental right to vote. One of the basic purposes of the Act is to increase the historically low registration rates of minorities and persons with disabilities that have resulted from discrimination. The Motor Voter Act requires all offices of State-funded programs that are primarily engaged in providing services to persons with disabilities to provide all program applicants with voter registration forms, to assist them in completing the forms, and to transmit completed forms to the appropriate State official. For more information, contact:

U.S. Department of Justice
Civil Rights Division
950 Pennsylvania Avenue, N.W.
Voting Section - 1800G
Washington, D.C. 20530

www.usdoj.gov/crt/voting

(800) 253-3931 (voice/TTY)

Civil Rights of Institutionalized Persons Act

The Civil Rights of Institutionalized Persons Act (CRIPA) authorizes the U.S. Attorney General to investigate conditions of confinement at State and local government institutions such as prisons, jails, pretrial detention centers, juvenile correctional facilities, publicly operated nursing homes, and institutions for people with psychiatric or developmental disabilities. Its purpose is to allow the Attorney General to uncover and correct widespread deficiencies that seriously jeopardize the health and safety of residents of institutions. The Attorney General does not have authority under CRIPA to investigate isolated incidents or to represent individual institutionalized persons. The Attorney General may initiate civil law suits where there is reasonable cause to believe that conditions are "egregious or flagrant," that they are subjecting residents to "grievous harm," and that they are part of a "pattern or practice" of resistance to residents' full enjoyment of constitutional or Federal rights, including title II of the ADA and section 504 of the Rehabilitation Act. For more information or to bring a matter to the Department of Justice's attention, contact:

> U.S. Department of Justice
> Civil Rights Division
> 950 Pennsylvania Avenue, N.W.
> Special Litigation Section - PHB
> Washington, D.C. 20530
>
> www.usdoj.gov/crt/split
>
> (877) 218-5228 (voice/TTY)

Individuals with Disabilities Education Act

The Individuals with Disabilities Education Act (IDEA) (formerly called P.L. 94-142 or the Education for all Handicapped Children Act of 1975) requires public schools to make available to all eligible children with disabilities a free appropriate public education in the least restrictive environment appropriate to their individual needs. IDEA requires public school systems to develop appropriate Individualized Education Programs (IEP's) for each child. The specific special education and related services outlined in each IEP reflect the individualized needs of each student. IDEA also mandates that particular procedures be followed in the development of the IEP. Each student's IEP must be developed by a team of knowledgeable persons and must be at least reviewed annually. The team includes the child's teacher; the parents, subject to certain limited exceptions; the child, if determined appropriate; an agency representative who is qualified to provide or supervise the provision of special education; and other individuals at the parents' or agency's discretion. If parents disagree with the proposed IEP, they can request a due process hearing and a review from the State educational agency if applicable in that state. They also can appeal the State agency's decision to State or Federal court. For more information, contact:

Office of Special Education & Rehabilitative Services
U.S. Department of Education
400 Maryland Avenue, S.W.
Washington, D.C. 20202-7100

www.ed.gov/about/offices/list/osers/osep

(202) 245-7468 (voice/TTY)

Rehabilitation Act

The Rehabilitation Act prohibits discrimination on the basis of disability in programs conducted by Federal agencies, in programs receiving Federal financial assistance, in Federal employment, and in the employment practices of Federal contractors. The standards for determining employment discrimination under the Rehabilitation Act are the same as those used in title I of the Americans with Disabilities Act.

Section 501

Section 501 requires affirmative action and nondiscrimination in employment by Federal agencies of the executive branch. To obtain more information or to file a complaint, employees should contact their agency's Equal Employment Opportunity Office.

Section 503

Section 503 requires affirmative action and prohibits employment discrimination by Federal government contractors and subcontractors with contracts of more than $10,000. For more information on section 503, contact:

Office of Federal Contract Compliance Programs
U.S. Department of Labor
200 Constitution Avenue, N.W., Room C-3325
Washington, D.C. 20210

www.dol.gov/esa/ofccp

(202) 693-0106 (voice/relay)

Section 504

Section 504 states that "no qualified individual with a disability in the United States shall be excluded from, denied the benefits of, or be subjected to discrimination under" any program or activity that either receives Federal financial assistance or is conducted by any Executive agency or the United States Postal Service. Each Federal agency has its own set of section 504 regulations that apply to its own programs. Agencies that provide Federal financial assistance also have section 504 regulations covering entities that receive Federal aid. Requirements common to these regulations include reasonable accommodation for employees with disabilities; program accessibility; effective communication with people who have hearing or vision disabilities; and accessible new construction and alterations. Each agency is responsible for enforcing its own regulations. Section 504 may also be enforced through private lawsuits. It is not necessary to file a complaint with a Federal agency or to receive a "right-to-sue" letter before going to court. For information on how to file 504 complaints with the appropriate agency, contact:

        U.S. Department of Justice
        Civil Rights Division
        950 Pennsylvania Avenue, N.W.
        Disability Rights Section - NYAV
        Washington, D.C. 20530

        www.ada.gov

        (800) 514-0301 (voice)
        (800) 514-0383 (TTY)

Section 508

Section 508 establishes requirements for electronic and information technology developed, maintained, procured, or used by the Federal government. Section 508 requires Federal electronic and information technology to be accessible to people with disabilities, including employees and members of the public. An accessible information technology system is one that can be operated in a variety of ways and does not rely on a single sense or ability of the user. For example, a system that provides output only in visual format may not be accessible to people with visual impairments and a system that provides output only in audio format may not be accessible to people who are deaf or hard of hearing. Some individuals with disabilities may need accessibility-related software or peripheral devices in order to use systems that comply with Section 508. For more information on section 508, contact:

U.S. General Services Administration
Center for IT Accommodation (CITA)
1800 F Street, N.W. Room 1234, MC:MKC
Washington, DC 20405-0001

www.gsa.gov/section508

(202) 501-4906 (voice)
(202) 501-2010 (TTY)

U.S. Architectural and Transportation
Barriers Compliance Board
1331 F Street, N.W., Suite 1000
Washington, DC 20004-1111

www.access-board.gov

800-872-2253 (voice)
800-993-2822 (TTY)

Architectural Barriers Act

The Architectural Barriers Act (ABA) requires that buildings and facilities that are designed, constructed, or altered with Federal funds, or leased by a Federal agency, comply with Federal standards for physical accessibility. ABA requirements are limited to architectural standards in new and altered buildings and in newly leased facilities. They do not address the activities conducted in those buildings and facilities. Facilities of the U.S. Postal Service are covered by the ABA. For more information or to file a complaint, contact:

U.S. Architectural and Transportation
Barriers Compliance Board
1331 F Street, N.W., Suite 1000
Washington, D.C. 20004-1111

www.access-board.gov

(800) 872-2253 (voice)
(800) 993-2822 (TTY)

General Sources of Disability Rights Information

ADA Information Line
(800) 514-0301 (voice)
(800) 514-0383 (TTY)

www.ada.gov

Regional ADA and IT
Technical Assistance Centers

(800) 949-4232 (voice/TTY)

www.adata.org

VOCABULARY RESOURCE MATERIALS

VOCABULARY WORD SEARCH Izzy, Willy-Nilly

```
L I N Z E R T O R T E D I B L E G L S D
P E A K E D C A T H E T E R R N S F U V
V N C O N T U S I O N S T K I K U B B Z
G E I H O B L I G E B K B D H Z O L T C
N G T T I N A V W X J U S F L R A L S
I O E W O L L A H S S R E E H P E N E R
S T H E R A P Y T D T O U C H E T D T H
S I T N I D M C K N A C B I T K S C Y A
E A S X O M D T I L B O Y D J I I Y L Z
R T O N U C G P J W I N C U A V O U Q M
P E R R S F D U A A L V N J E N B N W H
E R P A H Z V R N I I E E E C I G O S B
R B I C U E C K E L Z N G R F J T O E M
I I F V N M D N M I E I N P Y W D W R Z
N N Z I I I A A I N D E I V O L I O I A
C D L N V L J B A G S N T K B I M E O M
O E E E S M E V D I V T N P J B I S T B
M N R C R O L G O W D N O N E E N A R T
P T D R R D L N E S I M C J C R U V E N
E U J O G E E I N D H N R C T A T U P C
T R B S Z G P G T Q R E D K I T I L E Q
E E X I G V N I A A K M E L V E V S R Q
N D E S U O R G T L R D W N E D E E D Z
T I N D E F I N I T E Y G G J D F D J R
B O A S T I N G B A T I K S A R C A S M
```

ANEMIA	DECREPIT	INDENTURED	OBLIGE	STABILIZED
ANGORA	DIMINUTIVE	INTRUDING	PEAKED	SUBTLETY
AVULSED	DIVERT	JUVENILE	PREJUDICES	THERAPY
BANKRUPTCY	DWINDLED	KOWTOW	PRIVILEGED	TOUCHE
BATIK	EDIBLE	LIBERATED	PROSTHETIC	TRAUMA
BLAND	EVICT	LINZERTORTE	REPERTOIRE	VANITY
BOASTING	FIBULA	LIVERY	REPRESSING	WAILING
BOISTEROUS	GALE	NECROSIS	RUMMY	WOES
CATHETER	GENOISE	NEGOTIATE	SARCASM	
CONTINGENCY	GROUSED	NOTORIOUS	SHALLOW	
CONTUSIONS	INCOMPETENT	OBJECTIONS	SHEEN	
CONVENIENT	INDEFINITE	OBJECTIVE	SOLITARY	

VOCABULARY WORD SEARCH ANSWER KEY Izzy, Willy-Nilly

ANEMIA	DECREPIT	INDENTURED	OBLIGE	STABILIZED
ANGORA	DIMINUTIVE	INTRUDING	PEAKED	SUBTLETY
AVULSED	DIVERT	JUVENILE	PREJUDICES	THERAPY
BANKRUPTCY	DWINDLED	KOWTOW	PRIVILEGED	TOUCHE
BATIK	EDIBLE	LIBERATED	PROSTHETIC	TRAUMA
BLAND	EVICT	LINZERTORTE	REPERTOIRE	VANITY
BOASTING	FIBULA	LIVERY	REPRESSING	WAILING
BOISTEROUS	GALE	NECROSIS	RUMMY	WOES
CATHETER	GENOISE	NEGOTIATE	SARCASM	
CONTINGENCY	GROUSED	NOTORIOUS	SHALLOW	
CONTUSIONS	INCOMPETENT	OBJECTIONS	SHEEN	
CONVENIENT	INDEFINITE	OBJECTIVE	SOLITARY	

164

VOCABULARY CROSSWORD Izzy, Willy-Nilly

Across
2. Noisy and lively
4. Remove a tenant by legal procedures
9. Word used to acknowledge a successful point
11. Bruises
12. Shininess; brightness; luster
14. Having to do with the home or housekeeping
16. Strong wind
17. Obligation of people of high social position to behave kindly toward others: noblesse ___
19. Anything fit to be eaten
20. False perception of what one sees
21. Having a reduced red blood count resulting in paleness & weakness
22. Great sorrows or troubles
23. Long, pitiful crying
24. Show respect by kneeling and touching the ground with the forehead

Down
1. Holding back
2. Tasteless
3. Burning
5. Restored confidence
6. Card game
7. Uniform worn by servants or those in some particular group or trade
8. Forcing oneself upon others without being asked
10. Tube inserted into the body to drain urine from the bladder
11. Disapproved of strongly
13. Regard as perfect or more nearly perfect than is true
15. Lacking depth of character; superficial
18. Distract the attention of

VOCABULARY CROSSWORD ANSWER KEY   Izzy, Willy-Nilly Vocabulary

¹R				²B	O	I	S	T	E	R	O	³S	
⁴E	V	I	C	T							M		⁵R
P				L		⁶R		⁷L		⁸I		⁹T	O	¹⁰U	C	H	E
R			¹¹C	O	N	T	U	S	I	O	N	S		L		A		A
E			O		D		M		V		T			D		T		S
¹²S	H	E	E	N			M		E		R			E		H		S
S			D				Y		R		U			R		E		U
I		¹³I		E					Y		D			I		T		R
N		D	O	¹⁴M	E	¹⁵S	T	I	C		I			N		E		A
G		E		N		H					N			G		R		N
	¹⁶G	A	L	E		A		¹⁷O	B	L	I	G	E		¹⁸D			C
		L		D		L							¹⁹E	D	I	B	L	E
		I			²⁰I	L	L	U	S	I	O	N			V			
		Z				O							²¹A	N	E	M	I	A
²²W	O	E	S		²³W	A	I	L	I	N	G				R			
											²⁴K	O	W	T	O	W		

Across
2. Noisy and lively
4. Remove a tenant by legal procedures
9. Word used to acknowledge a successful point
11. Bruises
12. Shininess; brightness; luster
14. Having to do with the home or housekeeping
16. Strong wind
17. Obligation of people of high social position to behave kindly toward others: noblesse ___
19. Anything fit to be eaten
20. False perception of what one sees
21. Having a reduced red blood count resulting in paleness & weakness
22. Great sorrows or troubles
23. Long, pitiful crying
24. Show respect by kneeling and touching the ground with the forehead

Down
1. Holding back
2. Tasteless
3. Burning
5. Restored confidence
6. Card game
7. Uniform worn by servants or those in some particular group or trade
8. Forcing oneself upon others without being asked
10. Tube inserted into the body to drain urine from the bladder
11. Disapproved of strongly
13. Regard as perfect or more nearly perfect than is true
15. Lacking depth of character; superficial
18. Distract the attention of

VOCABULARY MATCHING 1 Izzy, Willy-Nilly

___ 1. INDEFINITE
___ 2. BLAND
___ 3. SHEEN
___ 4. PRIVILEGED
___ 5. DIMINUTIVE
___ 6. VANITY
___ 7. PSYCHOLOGICAL
___ 8. NEGOTIATE
___ 9. SHALLOW
___ 10. TRAUMA
___ 11. INDENTURED
___ 12. BATIK
___ 13. LIBERATED
___ 14. KOWTOW
___ 15. REPERTOIRE
___ 16. PRECONCEPTIONS
___ 17. RELUCTANCE
___ 18. NAUTILUS
___ 19. SUBTLETY
___ 20. RUMMY
___ 21. IDEALIZE
___ 22. CONVENIENT
___ 23. PROSTHETIC
___ 24. ILLUSION
___ 25. INCONVENIENT

A. Artificial replacement part of the body
B. ____ servant: one who is (voluntarily or not) committed to working for someone for a number of years
C. Of the mind; mental
D. Opinions formed in advance
E. Card game
F. Special skills, techniques, etc. of a particular person
G. Ability to be delicately suggestive
H. Lacking depth of character; superficial
I. Cloth decorated with dye--made by coating sections not to be dyed with removable wax
J. Having a right, advantage, or favor that is withheld from certain or all others
K. Tasteless
L. Regard as perfect or more nearly perfect than is true
M. Set free; released
N. Trademark for a kind of weight-lifting equipment
O. Unwillingness
P. Show respect by kneeling and touching the ground with the forehead
Q. Bargain or discuss in order to reach an agreement
R. Very small
S. Bodily injury, wound, or shock
T. Not precise or clear in meaning; vague
U. Not favorable to one's comfort; difficult to do
V. Easy to do, use or get to; easily accessible
W. Excessively proud of oneself of one's qualities or possessions
X. Shininess; brightness; luster
Y. False perception of what one sees

VOCABULARY MATCHING 1 ANSWER KEY Izzy, Willy-Nilly

T - 1. INDEFINITE
K - 2. BLAND
X - 3. SHEEN
J - 4. PRIVILEGED
R - 5. DIMINUTIVE
W 6. VANITY
C - 7. PSYCHOLOGICAL
Q - 8. NEGOTIATE
H - 9. SHALLOW
S - 10. TRAUMA
B - 11. INDENTURED
I - 12. BATIK
M - 13. LIBERATED
P - 14. KOWTOW
F - 15. REPERTOIRE
D - 16. PRECONCEPTIONS
O - 17. RELUCTANCE
N - 18. NAUTILUS
G - 19. SUBTLETY
E - 20. RUMMY
L - 21. IDEALIZE
V - 22. CONVENIENT
A - 23. PROSTHETIC
Y - 24. ILLUSION
U - 25. INCONVENIENT

A. Artificial replacement part of the body
B. ____ servant: one who is (voluntarily or not) committed to working for someone for a number of years
C. Of the mind; mental
D. Opinions formed in advance
E. Card game
F. Special skills, techniques, etc. of a particular person
G. Ability to be delicately suggestive
H. Lacking depth of character; superficial
I. Cloth decorated with dye--made by coating sections not to be dyed with removable wax
J. Having a right, advantage, or favor that is withheld from certain or all others
K. Tasteless
L. Regard as perfect or more nearly perfect than is true
M. Set free; released
N. Trademark for a kind of weight-lifting equipment
O. Unwillingness
P. Show respect by kneeling and touching the ground with the forehead
Q. Bargain or discuss in order to reach an agreement
R. Very small
S. Bodily injury, wound, or shock
T. Not precise or clear in meaning; vague
U. Not favorable to one's comfort; difficult to do
V. Easy to do, use or get to; easily accessible
W. Excessively proud of oneself of one's qualities or possessions
X. Shininess; brightness; luster
Y. False perception of what one sees

VOCABULARY MATCHING 2 Izzy, Willy-Nilly

___ 1. DWINDLED   A. Diminished; made less

___ 2. SOLITARY   B. Being alone

___ 3. PEAKED   C. Incapable; unskilled

___ 4. INCOMPETENT   D. Grumbled

___ 5. GROUSED   E. Disconnected

___ 6. IRRELEVANT   F. Not pertinent; not having anything to do with the matter at hand

___ 7. MARINATING   G. Serving to distract the attention

___ 8. HUMILIATION   H. Long, pitiful crying

___ 9. SHALLOW   I. Tube inserted into the body to drain urine from the bladder

___10. NOTORIOUS   J. Lacking depth of character; superficial

___11. GLYCERIN   K. Burning

___12. INADVERTENTLY   L. Thin and weak, as from illness

___13. SMOLDERING   M. Shininess; brightness; luster

___14. CATHETER   N. Having a right, advantage, or favor that is withheld from certain or all others

___15. DISJOINTED   O. Sets too low of an estimate or judgement

___16. LIBERATED   P. Odorless, colorless liquid used in skin lotion and other products

___17. UNDERESTIMATES   Q. Suspicion, intolerance, or irrational hatred of certain others

___18. PEDIATRICIAN   R. Feeling hurt pride or dignity being or seeming foolish

___19. SHEEN   S. Medical doctor specializing in the care of children

___20. WAILING   T. Unintentionally; without meaning to

___21. DIVERSIONARY   U. Soaking meat or fish in a mixture of spices or liquids prior to cooking

___22. PRECONCEPTIONS   V. Widely but unfavorably known

___23. PRIVILEGED   W. Opinions formed in advance

___24. PREJUDICES   X. Set free; released

___25. TOUCHE   Y. Word used to acknowledge a successful point

VOCABULARY MATCHING 2 ANSWER KEY Izzy, Willy-Nilly

A - 1. DWINDLED		A. Diminished; made less
B - 2. SOLITARY		B. Being alone
L - 3. PEAKED		C. Incapable; unskilled
C - 4. INCOMPETENT		D. Grumbled
D - 5. GROUSED		E. Disconnected
F - 6. IRRELEVANT		F. Not pertinent; not having anything to do with the matter at hand
U - 7. MARINATING		G. Serving to distract the attention
R - 8. HUMILIATION		H. Long, pitiful crying
J - 9. SHALLOW		I. Tube inserted into the body to drain urine from the bladder
V -10. NOTORIOUS		J. Lacking depth of character; superficial
P -11. GLYCERIN		K. Burning
T -12. INADVERTENTLY		L. Thin and weak, as from illness
K -13. SMOLDERING		M. Shininess; brightness; luster
I - 14. CATHETER		N. Having a right, advantage, or favor that is withheld from certain or all others
E -15. DISJOINTED		O. Sets too low of an estimate or judgement
X -16. LIBERATED		P. Odorless, colorless liquid used in skin lotion and other products
O -17. UNDERESTIMATES		Q. Suspicion, intolerance, or irrational hatred of certain others
S -18. PEDIATRICIAN		R. Feeling hurt pride or dignity being or seeming foolish
M -19. SHEEN		S. Medical doctor specializing in the care of children
H -20. WAILING		T. Unintentionally; without meaning to
G -21. DIVERSIONARY		U. Soaking meat or fish in a mixture of spices or liquids prior to cooking
W 22. PRECONCEPTIONS		V. Widely but unfavorably known
N -23. PRIVILEGED		W. Opinions formed in advance
Q -24. PREJUDICES		X. Set free; released
Y -25. TOUCHE		Y. Word used to acknowledge a successful point

VOCABULARY JUGGLE LETTERS 1 Izzy, Willy-Nilly

1. IDIINFTEEN = 1. _____
   Not precise or clear in meaning; vague

2. EVIDTR = 2. _____
   Distract the attention of

3. ASGCYPOLILCHO = 3. _____
   Of the mind; mental

4. TFEBLIREAIC = 4. _____
   Insane

5. IEVTC = 5. _____
   Remove a tenant by legal procedures

6. WEOS = 6. _____
   Great sorrows or troubles

7. IKSRHOEPS = 7. _____
   Small pastry turnovers with a filling

8. ODDEIISJNT = 8. _____
   Disconnected

9. DULSAEV = 9. _____
   Tore away by surgical traction

10. YRSAONVIRIED =10. _____
    Serving to distract the attention

11. NESIEOG =11. _____
    Rich, moist spongecake, often with a creamy filling between layers

12. NENVNOIETC =12. _____
    Easy to do, use or get to; easily accessible

13. EEPTRCDI =13. _____
    Worn out by old age

14. HYAAITCLLPEM =14. _____
    Done with emphasis or strength

15. TASYRLIO =15. _____
    Being alone

16. SRDIJUEECP =16. _____
Suspicion, intolerance, or irrational hatred of certain others

17. ABKIT =17. _____
Cloth decorated with dye--made by coating sections not to be dyed with removable wax

18. GIBTSOAN =18. _____
Bragging

19. GOARAN =19. _____
Soft yarn used for sweaters

20. EELIBD =20. _____
Anything fit to be eaten

21. ETLRNIAREV =21. _____
Not pertinent; not having anything to do with the matter at hand

22. IOATREISL =22. _____
Card game played by one person

23. RGVPELIEID =23. _____
Having a right, advantage, or favor that is withheld from certain or all others

24. EJVINEUL =24. _____
Characteristic of children

25. SRTIPETHCO =25. _____
Artificial replacement part of the body

26. CPNITNRCEPSOOE =26. _____
Opinions formed in advance

27. LNDTPEONEIE =27. _____
Embroidery of threads upon a canvas

28. UNAOIOGCJTNS =28. _____
Inflectional forms of verbs

29. KEEPAD =29. _____
Thin and weak, as from illness

30. YAVTNI =30. _____
Excessively proud of oneself of one's qualities or possessions

31. EIEPNTCMONT =31. _____
   Incapable; unskilled

32. EEGTONTAI =32. _____
   Bargain or discuss in order to reach an agreement

33. RIUSDNAMSTEEET =33. _____
   Sets too low of an estimate or judgement

34. NOBTOCIJSE =34. _____
   Reasons for disapproving or disliking

35. ESENH =35. _____
   Shininess; brightness; luster

36. ILBFAU =36. _____
   Long, thin outer bone of the human leg, between the knee and ankle

37. ANINTYLERDTEV =37. _____
   Unintentionally; without meaning to

38. IINUVDTEIM =38. _____
   Very small

39. AEGL =39. _____
   Strong wind

VOCABULARY JUGGLE LETTERS ANSWER KEY Izzy, Willy-Nilly

1. IDIINFTEEN = 1. INDEFINITE
   Not precise or clear in meaning; vague

2. EVIDTR = 2. DIVERT
   Distract the attention of

3. ASGCYPOLILCHO = 3. PSYCHOLOGICAL
   Of the mind; mental

4. TFEBLIREAIC = 4. CERTIFIABLE
   Insane

5. IEVTC = 5. EVICT
   Remove a tenant by legal procedures

6. WEOS = 6. WOES
   Great sorrows or troubles

7. IKSRHOEPS = 7. PEROSHKIS
   Small pastry turnovers with a filling

8. ODDEIISJNT = 8. DISJOINTED
   Disconnected

9. DULSAEV = 9. AVULSED
   Tore away by surgical traction

10. YRSAONVIRIED =10. DIVERSIONARY
    Serving to distract the attention

11. NESIEOG =11. GENOISE
    Rich, moist spongecake, often with a creamy filling between layers

12. NENVNOIETC =12. CONVENIENT
    Easy to do, use or get to; easily accessible

13. EEPTRCDI =13. DECREPIT
    Worn out by old age

14. HYAAITCLLPEM =14. EMPHATICALLY
    Done with emphasis or strength

15. TASYRLIO =15. SOLITARY
    Being alone

16. SRDIJUEECP =16. PREJUDICES

Suspicion, intolerance, or irrational hatred of certain others

17. ABKIT =17. BATIK

Cloth decorated with dye--made by coating sections not to be dyed with removable wax

18. GIBTSOAN =18. BOASTING

Bragging

19. GOARAN =19. ANGORA

Soft yarn used for sweaters

20. EELIBD =20. EDIBLE

Anything fit to be eaten

21. ETLRNIAREV =21. IRRELEVANT

Not pertinent; not having anything to do with the matter at hand

22. IOATREISL =22. SOLITAIRE

Card game played by one person

23. RGVPELIEID =23. PRIVILEGED

Having a right, advantage, or favor that is withheld from certain or all others

24. EJVINEUL =24. JUVENILE

Characteristic of children

25. SRTIPETHCO =25. PROSTHETIC

Artificial replacement part of the body

26. CPNITNRCEPSOOE =26. PRECONCEPTIONS

Opinions formed in advance

27. LNDTPEONEIE =27. NEEDLEPOINT

Embroidery of threads upon a canvas

28. UNAOIOGCJTNS =28. CONJUGATIONS

Inflectional forms of verbs

29. KEEPAD =29. PEAKED

Thin and weak, as from illness

30. YAVTNI =30. VANITY

Excessively proud of oneself of one's qualities or possessions

31. EIEPNTCMONT =31. INCOMPETENT
Incapable; unskilled

32. EEGTONTAI =32. NEGOTIATE
Bargain or discuss in order to reach an agreement

33. RIUSDNAMSTEEET =33. UNDERESTIMATES
Sets too low of an estimate or judgement

34. NOBTOCIJSE =34. OBJECTIONS
Reasons for disapproving or disliking

35. ESENH =35. SHEEN
Shininess; brightness; luster

36. ILBFAU =36. FIBULA
Long, thin outer bone of the human leg, between the knee and ankle

37. ANINTYLERDTEV =37. INADVERTENTLY
Unintentionally; without meaning to

38. IINUVDTEIM =38. DIMINUTIVE
Very small

39. AEGL =39. GALE
Strong wind

VOCABULARY JUGGLE LETTERS 2 Izzy, Willy-Nilly

1. SSERRIPGNE = 1. _____
   Holding back

2. NEAAMI = 2. _____
   Having a reduced red blood count resulting in paleness & weakness

3. EVRYLI = 3. _____
   Uniform worn by servants or those in some particular group or trade

4. RGUEDOS = 4. _____
   Grumbled

5. ONTIEVNECNIN = 5. _____
   Not favorable to one's comfort; difficult to do

6. ADNLB = 6. _____
   Tasteless

7. DNUNITRGI = 7. _____
   Forcing oneself upon others without being asked

8. IIRIEATDNCPA = 8. _____
   Medical doctor specializing in the care of children

9. DLIIAEZE = 9. _____
   Regard as perfect or more nearly perfect than is true

10. OUTHEC =10. _____
    Word used to acknowledge a successful point

11. DDLIDWNE =11. _____
    Diminished; made less

12. SRUTONOOI =12. _____
    Widely but unfavorably known

13. HLOLWSA =13. _____
    Lacking depth of character; superficial

14. BLSTTEYU =14. _____
    Ability to be delicately suggestive

15. TDEDFLEA =15. _____
    Made smaller or less important

16. ESRDMNGILO =16. _____
Burning

17. AARMUT =17. _____
Bodily injury, wound, or shock

18. UTLUIANS =18. _____
Trademark for a kind of weight-lifting equipment

19. EIORCNSS =19. _____
Death of decay of tissue in a part of the body

20. ECILYNGR =20. _____
Odorless, colorless liquid used in skin lotion and other products

21. RRNILTTOZEE =21. _____
Rich pastry made of almond dough & raspberry jam filling

22. TCHREETA =22. _____
Tube inserted into the body to drain urine from the bladder

23. EDNDUNRTEI =23. _____
____ servant: one who is (voluntarily or not) committed to working for someone for a number of years

24. MMYUR =24. _____
Card game

25. UHAOMTIIILN =25. _____
Feeling hurt pride or dignity being or seeming foolish

26. TPUDMATAE =26. _____
Cut off through surgery

27. TCNRPYKBAU =27. _____
State of being unable to pay debts

28. EENMDDNOC =28. _____
Disapproved of strongly

29. BOGLIE =29. _____
Obligation of people of high social position to behave kindly toward others: noblesse ___

30. OSUSCOTNNI =30. _____
Bruises

31. ECOSDTIM =31. _____
Having to do with the home or housekeeping

32. TIZLSAIBDE =32. _____
Kept from changing

33. ZNOGAATIEN =33. _____
Oppose; struggle against

34. ETHAPYR =34. _____
Physical ___: treatment of injury by physical means rather than with drugs

35. NEIITSTYN =35. _____
Great energy of emotion, thought, or activity

36. OYTNICNCGNE =36. _____
A possible, unforeseen, or accidental occurrence

37. UEBIRSTSOO =37. _____
Noisy and lively

38. CELECATNRU =38. _____
Unwillingness

39. ARITAIMNGN =39. _____
Soaking meat or fish in a mixture of spices or liquids prior to cooking

VOCABULARY JUGGLE LETTERS 2 ANSWER KEY Izzy, Willy-Nilly

1. SSERRIPGNE = 1. REPRESSING
   Holding back

2. NEAAMI = 2. ANEMIA
   Having a reduced red blood count resulting in paleness & weakness

3. EVRYLI = 3. LIVERY
   Uniform worn by servants or those in some particular group or trade

4. RGUEDOS = 4. GROUSED
   Grumbled

5. ONTIEVNECNIN = 5. INCONVENIENT
   Not favorable to one's comfort; difficult to do

6. ADNLB = 6. BLAND
   Tasteless

7. DNUNITRGI = 7. INTRUDING
   Forcing oneself upon others without being asked

8. IIRIEATDNCPA = 8. PEDIATRICIAN
   Medical doctor specializing in the care of children

9. DLIIAEZE = 9. IDEALIZE
   Regard as perfect or more nearly perfect than is true

10. OUTHEC =10. TOUCHE
    Word used to acknowledge a successful point

11. DDLIDWNE =11. DWINDLED
    Diminished; made less

12. SRUTONOOI =12. NOTORIOUS
    Widely but unfavorably known

13. HLOLWSA =13. SHALLOW
    Lacking depth of character; superficial

14. BLSTTEYU =14. SUBTLETY
    Ability to be delicately suggestive

15. TDEDFLEA =15. DEFLATED
    Made smaller or less important

16. ESRDMNGILO =16. SMOLDERING
Burning

17. AARMUT =17. TRAUMA
Bodily injury, wound, or shock

18. UTLUIANS =18. NAUTILUS
Trademark for a kind of weight-lifting equipment

19. EIORCNSS =19. NECROSIS
Death of decay of tissue in a part of the body

20. ECILYNGR =20. GLYCERIN
Odorless, colorless liquid used in skin lotion and other products

21. RRNILTTOZEE =21. LINZERTORTE
Rich pastry made of almond dough & raspberry jam filling

22. TCHREETA =22. CATHETER
Tube inserted into the body to drain urine from the bladder

23. EDNDUNRTEI =23. INDENTURED
____ servant: one who is (voluntarily or not) committed to working for someone for a number of years

24. MMYUR =24. RUMMY
Card game

25. UHAOMTIIILN =25. HUMILIATION
Feeling hurt pride or dignity being or seeming foolish

26. TPUDMATAE =26. AMPUTATED
Cut off through surgery

27. TCNRPYKBAU =27. BANKRUPTCY
State of being unable to pay debts

28. EENMDDNOC =28. CONDEMNED
Disapproved of strongly

29. BOGLIE =29. OBLIGE
Obligation of people of high social position to behave kindly toward others: noblesse ___

30. OSUSCOTNNI =30. CONTUSIONS
Bruises

31. ECOSDTIM =31. DOMESTIC
Having to do with the home or housekeeping

32. TIZLSAIBDE =32. STABILIZED
Kept from changing

33. ZNOGAATIEN =33. ANTAGONIZE
Oppose; struggle against

34. ETHAPYR =34. THERAPY
Physical ___: treatment of injury by physical means rather than with drugs

35. NEIITSTYN =35. INTENSITY
Great energy of emotion, thought, or activity

36. OYTNICNCGNE =36. CONTINGENCY
A possible, unforeseen, or accidental occurrence

37. UEBIRSTSOO =37. BOISTEROUS
Noisy and lively

38. CELECATNRU =38. RELUCTANCE
Unwillingness

39. ARITAIMNGN =39. MARINATING
Soaking meat or fish in a mixture of spices or liquids prior to cooking

Izzy, Willy-Nilly Vocabulary Word List

No.	Word	Clue/Definition
1.	AMPUTATED	Cut off through surgery
2.	ANEMIA	Having a reduced red blood count resulting in paleness & weakness
3.	ANGORA	Soft yarn used for sweaters
4.	ANTAGONIZE	Oppose; struggle against
5.	AVULSED	Tore away by surgical traction
6.	BANKRUPTCY	State of being unable to pay debts
7.	BATIK	Cloth decorated with dye--made by coating sections not to be dyed with removable wax
8.	BLAND	Tasteless
9.	BOASTING	Bragging
10.	BOISTEROUS	Noisy and lively
11.	CATHETER	Tube inserted into the body to drain urine from the bladder
12.	CERTIFIABLE	Insane
13.	CONDEMNED	Disapproved of strongly
14.	CONJUGATIONS	Inflectional forms of verbs
15.	CONTINGENCY	A possible, unforeseen, or accidental occurrence
16.	CONTUSIONS	Bruises
17.	CONVENIENT	Easy to do, use or get to; easily accessible
18.	DECREPIT	Worn out by old age
19.	DEFLATED	Made smaller or less important
20.	DIMINUTIVE	Very small
21.	DISJOINTED	Disconnected
22.	DIVERSIONARY	Serving to distract the attention
23.	DIVERT	Distract the attention of
24.	DOMESTIC	Having to do with the home or housekeeping
25.	DWINDLED	Diminished; made less
26.	EDIBLE	Anything fit to be eaten
27.	EMPHATICALLY	Done with emphasis or strength
28.	EVICT	Remove a tenant by legal procedures
29.	FIBULA	Long, thin outer bone of the human leg, between the knee and ankle
30.	GALE	Strong wind
31.	GENOISE	Rich, moist spongecake, often with a creamy filling between layers
32.	GLYCERIN	Odorless, colorless liquid used in skin lotion and other products
33.	GROUSED	Grumbled
34.	HUMILIATION	Feeling hurt pride or dignity being or seeming foolish
35.	IDEALIZE	Regard as perfect or more nearly perfect than is true
36.	ILLUSION	False perception of what one sees
37.	INADVERTENTLY	Unintentionally; without meaning to
38.	INCOMPETENT	Incapable; unskilled
39.	INCONVENIENT	Not favorable to one's comfort; difficult to do
40.	INDEFINITE	Not precise or clear in meaning; vague
41.	INDENTURED	____ servant: one who is (voluntarily or not) committed to working for someone for a number of years
42.	INTENSITY	Great energy of emotion, thought, or activity
43.	INTRUDING	Forcing oneself upon others without being asked
44.	IRRELEVANT	Not pertinent; not having anything to do with the matter at hand
45.	JUVENILE	Characteristic of children
46.	KOWTOW	Show respect by kneeling and touching the ground with the forehead

Izzy, Willy-Nilly Vocabulary Word List Continued

No.	Word	Clue/Definition
47.	LIBERATED	Set free; released
48.	LINZERTORTE	Rich pastry made of almond dough & raspberry jam filling
49.	LIVERY	Uniform worn by servants or those in some particular group or trade
50.	MARINATING	Soaking meat or fish in a mixture of spices or liquids prior to cooking
51.	NAUTILUS	Trademark for a kind of weight-lifting equipment
52.	NECROSIS	Death of decay of tissue in a part of the body
53.	NEEDLEPOINT	Embroidery of threads upon a canvas
54.	NEGOTIATE	Bargain or discuss in order to reach an agreement
55.	NOTORIOUS	Widely but unfavorably known
56.	OBJECTIONS	Reasons for disapproving or disliking
57.	OBJECTIVE	Without bias or prejudice
58.	OBLIGE	Obligation of people of high social position to behave kindly toward others: noblesse ___
59.	PEAKED	Thin and weak, as from illness
60.	PEDIATRICIAN	Medical doctor specializing in the care of children
61.	PEROSHKIS	Small pastry turnovers with a filling
62.	PRECONCEPTIONS	Opinions formed in advance
63.	PREJUDICES	Suspicion, intolerance, or irrational hatred of certain others
64.	PRIVILEGED	Having a right, advantage, or favor that is withheld from certain or all others
65.	PROSTHETIC	Artificial replacement part of the body
66.	PSYCHOLOGICAL	Of the mind; mental
67.	REASSURANCE	Restored confidence
68.	RELUCTANCE	Unwillingness
69.	REPERTOIRE	Special skills, techniques, etc. of a particular person
70.	REPRESSING	Holding back
71.	RUMMY	Card game
72.	SARCASM	A taunting or cutting remark
73.	SHALLOW	Lacking depth of character; superficial
74.	SHEEN	Shininess; brightness; luster
75.	SMOLDERING	Burning
76.	SOLITAIRE	Card game played by one person
77.	SOLITARY	Being alone
78.	STABILIZED	Kept from changing
79.	SUBTLETY	Ability to be delicately suggestive
80.	THERAPY	Physical ___: treatment of injury by physical means rather than with drugs
81.	TOUCHE	Word used to acknowledge a successful point
82.	TRAUMA	Bodily injury, wound, or shock
83.	UNDERESTIMATES	Sets too low of an estimate or judgement
84.	VANITY	Excessively proud of oneself of one's qualities or possessions
85.	WAILING	Long, pitiful crying
86.	WOES	Great sorrows or troubles

www.ingramcontent.com/pod-product-compliance
Lightning Source LLC
Chambersburg PA
CBHW051406070526
44584CB00023B/3314